SECRETS
AND LIES

SECRETS AND LIES

SAM FAIERS

MICHAEL JOSEPH
an imprint of
PENGUIN BOOKS

MICHAEL JOSEPH

UK | USA | Canada | Ireland | Australia
India | New Zealand | South Africa

Michael Joseph is part of the Penguin Random House group of companies
whose addresses can be found at global.penguinrandomhouse.com.

First published 2015

001

Text copyright © Sam Faiers, 2015
See page 280 for photography copyright

The moral right of the author has been asserted

Set in 13/18pt Minion Pro
Typeset by Penguin Books
Printed in Great Britain by Clays Ltd, St Ives plc

A CIP catalogue record for this book is available from the British Library

ISBN: 978–1–405–92117–6

To my beautiful niece, Nelly
You have brought so much joy to our family
and I love you so much

Contents

Prologue –
The Break-up

pressed 'send' and that was it. One simple text and it was over. There were no tears – in fact, I felt weirdly numb and exhausted.

I had finally had enough and I knew it had to be done, for the sake of my sanity and health if nothing else. Me and Joey, the cute Essex couple, were through for good. When we got back together for the final time after my Crohn's was diagnosed, there was no doubt I hoped it would end in marriage and children. I truly thought we had both grown up enough to have the 'happy ever after'. But here I was, ending the fairy tale via text message. I was so tired – tired of pretending that this relationship had legs and it felt good to finally be taking charge of the situation. I felt strong. I had tried to call him but he didn't answer – that wasn't unusual, he quite often did that. At this time we were barely speaking, let alone seeing each other. So when he didn't pick up, I sent him a text. Then, when he didn't answer that, I sent him an email as I didn't want there to be any doubt that I was serious about us being over. I did this first thing in the morning and it took him all day to respond. When he finally did decide to acknowledge it, he called the house phone, which I then ignored. I needed to stay focussed. I knew he had read my message and that if we spoke now, we would just cry. I didn't want to answer and then change my mind and go back around in circles again and again. We would go back to square one again. This was it.

For once, there was no huge *TOWIE*-type screaming match with cameras and lights and, for that, I was glad. We had spent most of our on–off four-year relationship like that, trying to have real feelings in a staged and set-up situation where the producer's wishes for a scandal or a headline-worthy melt-down came before ours. So now that it was just me in charge of my life was a relief.

I was done with Joey Essex. I was sick of all the fights and, truth be told, I just didn't know who Joey was any more – I didn't want to keep trying to find out as I wasn't sure I'd like what I found.

Our love for each other when we were together was never in question and there was always such powerful chemistry. The trouble was the non-stop rows and the fact that I never knew which Joey I was going to get. He lost his mum at a young age and suffered hugely from not having her around. My mum is my world so I can't imagine what it must be like to not have her there to hug you and tell you it will be okay. He needed someone to tell it to him straight when he was messing up and he didn't have those people around him. His manager Dave Read, and his family, Chloe Sims, Frankie Essex – they aren't tough or direct with him. He is like Peter

Pan, frozen in time and unable to handle anything bad or real, and that included the reality of us. Every couple rows, that's life, but with Joey it was always the end of the world and he could never keep anything private. It was bad enough sharing our ups and downs with thousands of viewers, but that wasn't enough for him. He had to tell his whole family every time we so much as disagreed. Every row was twisted to make me look like the bad one. The truth is that he gave as good as he got, he played games and messed with my head all the time, but Joey has this need to be loved and always be in the right. This need is so deep-rooted that it stops him being honest with himself about anything.

Don't get me wrong, I am no saint. I am fiery and a party girl, but, at heart, I am all about my family. They come first, always, and when I have a boyfriend, he is part of that too. I work hard, play hard, but I love and respect hard too, and Joey knew that. I had always accepted Joey for what he was, but he changed. He went from lovable Joey who used to get a bit tipsy and silly, who used to knock on my mum's door at 3 a.m. after a PA [public appearance] declaring his love for everyone and making us all laugh – he went from that to a Joey I didn't recognize. The guy who towards the end thought his phone was being bugged, that people were out to get him and dig him out, the guy who went through my phone obsessively and demanded that I unfollow people on Twitter, including old friends. We both were as bad as each other and I found myself at times towards the end looking through his phone. He partied too much, got led astray too much and he got so jealous.

He was so edgy, jittery, angry and frustrated it was like a split personality followed by days of paranoia. I didn't know what to do or what to make of the situation. The last time we rekindled things we had both left the show that made us famous, and I thought we had a shot, I really did. But demons stay put until they are dealt with and sometimes, no matter how much you love someone, you can't fix them and you can't make yourself compatible with them. For four years we had complete trust, towards the end sadly that wasn't the case.

Anyway, more of that later. In that moment when I sent that text ending things, I felt utter relief. Obviously I was sad too as I loved him to bits and we had spent a long time planning our future, but I was relieved. I had taken control and put myself first. After a year of being so ill that I had no idea what was wrong with me, a year of more drama than anyone knew, I couldn't do it any more. I didn't want to do it any more.

I pressed 'send' and didn't know what to do with myself. I knew I just had to get away from it all. So I booked the next flight to LA in a bid to heal my broken heart and rediscover the old me.

> Hi, I know your not going to call me back anytime soon. I am going to walk away. I'm going away tomorrow to get my head clear. I love you so much, but I'm not prepared to sit back and watch u ruin your life. No matter if I have been drunk in the past and started arguments, u have controlled me & treated me really bad for some time now.

PROLOGUE – THE BREAK-UP

You have disrespected my family to my face. You tell everyone u don't like me and your finished with me (including Nikki webber). You foul mouth me to everyone, and that's just not fair.

You are always up and down, your paranoid & blame every-thing on me. Dave rules your life & going out is a priority and money. I'm a minor thing that u just think u can keep there and pick up and drop me whenever u like. I don't deserve to be treated like that when all I do is try. I'm always trying so hard to make time for each other.

You don't want me. U got back with me when I was ill because u felt sorry for me, and yours and Amy's relationship come to an end.

You can use those pictures against me and say what u want to the press. But deep down We both know its nothing to do with it. I am not going to say anything to the press.

I'm deeply heartbroken.
I love u and wish u all the best.

Bye
Love u

1

Fame and *TOWIE*

How It All Began

I t really gets on my nerves the way everyone thinks people from Essex are thick. It is such a cliché. I don't kid myself. I know I am not an award-winning actress and that I am in the public eye because of a reality TV show, and I will always be grateful for that, but I come from a good family and I work hard – not all people from Essex are brash, materialistic and chavvy. I certainly never really imagined being famous. It is well documented how I found my way on to *TOWIE* in the first place. You can still find the first comedy pilot on YouTube – as Amy Childs comes out through the changing-room curtain wearing this enormous wedding dress, me and Harry Derbidge wetting ourselves laughing at my comment that Kirk was bound to 'take her up the aisle' dressed like that. We were hysterical! It didn't bode well for our big TV-screen moment. We got into a lot of trouble with the producers but, even though it was a brilliant moment (and there were many more where that came from), it didn't take long for me to wise up.

Truth was that a month before that first TV pilot clip, I'd been doing a nine-to-five job in the Lloyds TSB bank in Ilford and pinning all my hopes of making some decent money on my glamour-modelling career. Even then, it wasn't fame I was after and it wasn't like taking my top off was my idea of the best career ladder I could climb. Back then I wanted to save for the future as well as have money to buy nice things. I don't think there is anything wrong in admitting that. I think it is a good example to work hard and strive for the life I want for myself and, if I'm lucky enough, for my kids in the future. I know the score – this could end tomorrow and I work hard every day to make sure I am secure for life. When kids come along, I want to be there for them all the time and having money will obviously help me do that. Don't get me wrong, I will work hard and show them mummies can have jobs and still be there for them, but in ten years' time I don't want to be on the front of magazines as they discuss the new diet I am supposed to be following or if I have put on five pounds. (It always amazes me how they get away with claiming this. I mean, are they there when I get on the scales?!) What I do, I do because I love it and I like to think that people will keep supporting me and making my fragrances, clothing lines, lashes, books, etc. a success because they know how hard I work and they like what I do and what I stand for. I was brought up by my mum to believe that you get out what you put in and I truly believe that – me and Billie both do – and that was my motto whilst on the show and in everything I have done since.

I am not like some from the show (Arg, I am talking about you!) who aren't professional, turn up late or turn up still drunk after a massive night (I love you really, James). Although filming the show was great fun, I also saw it for what it was – and that's a job to be taken seriously. I signed a contract and had obligations. Admittedly, in the early days it was more fun and I was more immature – of course I was. I was so young. It was new and exciting and I was being paid to be on camera. It is so hard to convey that buzz I got from the early days. I will never forget the *TOWIE* launch night when I had my hair and nails done and the producers sent a car to collect me, Amy and Kirk to take us from Essex to the Maddox Club in London. It was the first moment I felt excited about how different my life could be. There were journalists and paps and everything. It was a world away from Brentwood High Street, my Saturday job, my role at the bank and working out what outfit I was going to wear clubbing on a Saturday night. It was life-changing and it didn't really feel like a job. That said, the first myth about being on the show was that it made us a lot of money – we didn't get paid as much as you think!

At the beginning we started off with £50 a day for filming and most reality TV stars barely get that. It quickly became clear to me that my main earnings wouldn't come from the show, hence why I have always made the most of my opportunities away from the camera. Be sensible whilst it is there was always my thinking and I knew that staying on the show for as long as possible opened those exciting doors for me. I quickly lined up as many personal appearances as I could and then followed with things like magazine deals, columns, product placements, endorsements, branding and television work. Once that was established, I was lucky enough to get my first book deal – I was actually the first *TOWIE* member to publish a book about what it was like behind the scenes. I certainly didn't hold back, although it was slightly awkward that I had commented on Joey's ability in bed and we had just got back together at the time of publication! It got to number one and I know my mum was so proud of me. I worked hard going to book signings up and down the country and it really paid off when I knocked Simon Cowell's book off the top spot! It was also a great way to thank the loyal fans who queued up to get books and T-shirts signed – I never underestimate they are the reason I am here. What I loved most of all was seeing young girls and their mums in the queue – to me that meant I must be doing something right. Young girls wanted to be like me and their mums supported that and saw me as a good role model – that meant the world to me. I know that I have a responsibility to be the best person I can be and set a good example and I won't ever forget that. I suppose that's why I am so vocal about those who are in the public eye and don't set the right example. Rightly or wrongly, people in the public eye, on TV and in magazines are looked up to and followed. So, with that in mind, don't disrespect women and don't use foul language and cause aggravation for the sake of it. Remember that you are being watched and people are looking up to you.

Filming hours for the show were almost criminal, sensible people kept their real paid jobs throughout the series, though time frames made it hard. We would sit for hours on end in tiny, stuffy rooms waiting to be called for our scenes. A lot of the time you were stuck in impossibly small spaces with people you couldn't stand, which made things awkward and allowed for tempers to fray.

Unless you are someone like Lauren Conrad, you don't actually earn cash directly from the show. At the start we all signed contracts with the production company Lime saying that once we left the show, for the first four months after our departure, we would give 15 per cent of our earnings to the show. The logic behind this, we were told, was that we wouldn't have any of this other work if it hadn't been for the show as that was why we were famous.

But *TOWIE* was a relaxed set-up at the start thanks to the people who were in charge back in the day. Sarah Dillistone, who worked at Lime, was a godsend. I completely trusted her with my life (which was just as well as I, in effect, signed it over to the producers). She was often dispatched to come round to our houses and keep a close eye on us – it was her job to know everything about us so that she could decide which bits would make good TV, but she was a laugh and took the time to get to know us all and what made us tick. So I guess you could call it 'dramality', but it was much more organic – she certainly never suggested staging anything that wasn't real, nor did she suggest that they treat us more like *Big Brother* contestants by playing dirty tricks and deliberately stirring situations to wind people up and goad them into bad behaviour. It was definitely much less manipulated than it is now. Editing is reality TV's best weapon and, in all honesty, editing is what makes *TOWIE*. There is a whole suite for the editors to cut, splice, edit all scenes, conversations, 'impromptu meetings' and VTs to add drama and make them so much bitchier and dramatic. It takes hours of filming to get those action-packed forty-five minutes that end up being aired. All those comedy lingering looks and ridiculous pauses as people fall out, they are all manipulated.

The truth is that, especially since I left, there have been some recent scenes that just felt really uncomfortable to watch, like when Jess and Ricky broke up in Series 13. They clearly couldn't stand to be near each other. Jess was properly hurting after what Ricky had done; I mean, nothing against Ricky, but talking about your sex life on TV and calling your ex 'boring' just after you've broken up is not cool. Obviously being on a show like *TOWIE* it is warts and all. You can't have the good but then shy away from the bad. It isn't how it works, it is all or nothing. Yet it looked so raw that I couldn't watch. It was all still obviously painful and it is so hard when the first time you are addressing something real in your relationship, it is with a camera in your face. It can cause a lot of damage. Believe me, I know. I was so concerned about Jess and how she was after this had all happened that she came away with us to Dubai in November 2014. Jess is a good friend and I wanted to make sure she was okay.

And I don't mind holding my hand up and saying that the original cast were head and shoulders above some of the lot they have on there now. The original point of the show was a warm-hearted and candid look at the real lives of some lovable characters who got themselves into scrapes that were harmless and funny. We all loved each other, came from good homes, liked to party a bit at Sugar Hut, but were well brought up. I know I sound like an old woman, but don't they worry about what their family will say when they watch them on screen behaving like that? I know what my mum would say! But I am well aware that producers have far more say than characters in reality TV shows. You can argue until you are blue in the face about something you do or don't want to do, but the ultimate decision is theirs. The only aim is to make great TV. I would say the same applies to shows like *Celebrity Big Brother* too – my illness was never shown as it wasn't the vibe they wanted. People forget that a lot of care is put into generating headlines and PR before the launch of a new series – stories are strategically placed by the *TOWIE* publicity team and characters are encouraged to build intrigue on Twitter by rowing and digging each other out. It all heightens that sense of drama and anticipation. I am fully aware that the priority is good TV, that's what we all signed up for and I would never moan about that. Obviously anything that heightens the sense of drama and anticipation is welcomed by the producers and they do all they can to aid that. Then there are some characters who feel they need more airtime so they create their own angles and dramas.

Of course everyone who joins the show knows that the producers hire people with a strategy in mind. Characters who explode on screen and cause ructions are no accident, they know why they are there and they deliver the required drama. Of course producers want Gemma to get wound up and scream at people and make them cry, they want her to row with softer people like Harry and Bobby so they will break down, they want her and Ferne to fight and hold grudges. It is all thought out and with personalities like Gemma, they know exactly which buttons to press. Like Mario, she has been guilty of forgetting where the line is between the show and her real life. I hope that changes a bit for her now that Charlie has taken some time out from the show to concentrate on his business. He's back now after a much needed rest but extracting himself from the war between Ferne and Chloe was the only real chance their relationship had of surviving.

The key to the success of the first series was that we mostly knew each other before the show began, so that meant an immediate chemistry and shorthand that worked on screen without it feeling forced. Me and Amy were particularly close but the original clan was me, Kirk Norcross, Amy, Arg, Jess Wright, Lauren Goodger, Harry Derbidge and Mark Wright. It was so much more straightforward back then: we weren't briefed – they left us to it and told us to act naturally and chat, drink and get ready for a night out, just like we normally would (except with cameras in every corner!). They filmed us walking Amy's dog in the park, us in Sugar Hut, just normal everyday stuff that helped the characters feel real and down to earth. On the last series I did there was a crew of forty plus for scenes. When I was filming at my house once with Ferne, Billie and Elliott they totally took over as there are so many. I suppose that is a sign of the show's success.

It was so hard to 'act normally'. People who say you forget the cameras are there after a while are lying – it is impossible!

What with the cameramen, the sound guys, the tripods, the director, the producer, etc., it definitely felt like a proper set rather than any real life I was used to! The idea back in Series 1 was not to have to reshoot any scenes and keep it as real as possible. We did small things like re-do a strut down the street or some lingering looks that they could use to splice into various scenes, but what they were after were genuine reactions. But now everyone talks about what is going on before an episode is filmed, nothing is a surprise. The rule at *TOWIE* was that there was supposed to be no contact between those filming before a scene so that it looked fresh and 'real'. I heard of times from other cast members where individuals had tried to assert their authority and force their way. I never took part in anything like this as I don't agree this is how it should be. Sometimes there were double bluffs – people would agree off camera to do one thing and then, when the filming started, they would completely change their mind. That was the worst and certainly what happened to me and Joey during the last bit of his time on the show, I never knew where I was with him in his last series. I know that was how Lucy felt that Mario behaved, as he became more arrogant and treated her terribly. It almost crushed her as he kept going back on what he said he really meant and changing the goal posts. It is so cruel to do that to someone you are engaged to, never mind on screen so that you are publicly humiliated. Not knowing where you stand is the most exhausting thing to deal with. I know that Lucy felt that one of the reasons she had to leave the show in the end was how it made her look – all she did was cry and take Mario back on screen after he humiliated her repeatedly, and that's not the girl I knew or grew up with. She would cry on me and Billie and we just wanted to tell her to bin Mario and have more respect for herself, but it wasn't our place – I wouldn't even interfere in any of Billie's relationships and she is my sister! Likewise, Billie never got involved in me and Joey's ups and downs either, some things are private. It also means that if you reserve judgement, you leave the door open to support that person when it does eventually go wrong. Lucy is smarter than that and she came to realize what was good for her in the end. She was so young when she joined the show and did her growing up on screen in front of the cameras, but she figured it out in the end and was definitely right to walk away. Like me, she never wanted to do anything on screen that embarrassed those she loved and I think there are only so many episodes your parents can watch you being mugged off. She started to find it difficult that they were embarrassed and that was that. It was definitely the best career move she has made. When I was in *Celebrity Big Brother*, Casey's mum coming in and telling her that the nation was watching Lee 'mug her off' will be one of my favourite reality TV moments ever. I'm sure that's what Lucy's parents felt like doing many a time throughout her time on the *TOWIE*! I only ever came close to that once, when Joey dumped me on the show.

By the time I left it felt more like a soap, where there were re-takes galore, where people were talking to each other about upcoming scenes in advance when they shouldn't and, frankly, where the producers played us all off against each other, knowing it would cause ructions. That particularly affected me and Joey in Series 9 when we were in Marbella when the producers deliberately put the boys and girls in separate hotels, knowing that Joey and I were in a tricky place in our relationship and what it would do to us. But more of that later.

It was such a different world to be in and it took a lot of getting used to. I know it looks like a laugh a minute, but it is actually really hard work. The filming days are long – they can be up to sixteen hours – and it is impossible to make any plans once you know the dates for the filming of the show – they would normally make you block out ten to twelve weeks at a time, so that meant no holidays, family weddings or christenings or anything that made you unavailable or meant you had to spend large amounts of time with people who weren't in the show. At the beginning we were given the dates that the show would air and told to keep those free and to go about our business as usual – however, we did have to remember that, as we lived our daily lives, we had to be mindful about living in a way and doing things that made us interesting to the producers. The show always came first, even if it meant breaking long-standing plans at the last minute to film a crowd scene in Sugar Hut or give them footage in Minnies. At this time we became inundated with work offers and couldn't do a lot because obviously filming came first. To add to the diary annoyance, we would often only get twelve hours' notice if we were needed, which often meant letting people down. Friends I had outside of the show did lose patience after a while, I suppose that's another reason the cast all stuck together so tightly, only we knew what it was really like and how hard it could be.

Another thing that is a favourite of producers is using our homes for filming. For example, they have been using Billie and Greg's house a lot since Nelly was born as Billie wants to stay in as much as she can and fit filming around Nelly. That said, it is comedy when they are filming a 'girls' night in' at 9 a.m. in Billie's living room and have stapled up black-out blinds to make it look like night-time. I've heard rumours that wine bottles were being opened by 9.30 a.m.! We don't get paid when they use our places and there can be a lot of damage done by people traipsing in and out with loads of filming equipment. As time has gone on more and more of the scenes are being done at cast members' homes, but there are some houses that aren't used. For example, we never went into my mum's house when I was on the show, even when Joey was filmed picking me up from there on our date. Lauren Pope doesn't really use her place and Arg has only just got a flat so we will see how often that is used before it becomes too much of a boy tip! That said, it took him months to actually move in. I feel for him, he was one of the very first cast members, and to leave under a cloud as he did would be really sad for him as I know how much he loves the show.

There has also been a lot of stick for the fact that some filming doesn't actually take place in Brentwood and producers are moving further out to places like Wanstead. I suppose it was inevitable that they would run out of places in Brentwood, there are only so many scenes you can do at Sugar Hut before it becomes boring. I think it is a good thing for local businesses – for example, Sumo Fresh in Wanstead is pretty much packed out all the time now since it started being used regularly for filming and that can only be a good thing. *TOWIE* has done wonders for local business, we all have a lot to be thankful for.

The key was to remember to be filmable at all times and that can make it hard not to get swept up in the bubble of it all as you start living your life in a studied way and focussed on the wrong things. You can start to only want to spend time with people you know will make you interesting to the show – and that is a recipe for disaster. As the show went on, that need to be 'interesting' very quickly paved the way for some of the more fame-hungry cast members to go out of their way to create their own dramas. It also became increasingly clear that having a boyfriend who wasn't on the show meant that you were bypassed for some of the juicier storylines involving other cast members. Whatever way you look at it, you always get more airtime if you are involved in an on-screen love triangle, whatever the show you are in, and some people took that to the limit, though it has progressively got worse as the show has gone on. It is very easy to spot the people who are desperate for the exposure and limelight, especially in the current series and with newer people.

For me, the first two series will always hold a dear place in my heart – it was before we could really measure the impact of being in the public eye. It was more like me, Amy and Harry out on one long jolly but with the cameras in tow. I can honestly say that we were just all truly ourselves in that series and I know that is when everyone really fell in love with Amy. She was sweet and funny and had no side to her at all; she would do anything for you. It was a shame that she was the first to be 'turned' by fame – you could see it in the fact that she left the show after Series 2 – she became managed by Can Associates who had previously looked after Katie Price. I don't think Amy leaving after Series 2 did her any favours. Amy did *Celebrity Big Brother* which went well for her, but her own show *All About Amy* on Channel 5 didn't do as well. She then went on *The Jump* on Channel 4, which Joey then won the following year. Amy is still a good friend of mine and Billie's but sadly we don't see her as much as we would like to or as much as we used to.

Essex Hotspots

It must have been good for Brentwood since the show started, there has been such recognition that trade for shops and bars has been brilliant, but I know some people feel like the show has taken over a normal little town and made it the most famous town in Essex. Brentwood is always booming at weekends, they even do *TOWIE* Tours which take you to all the shops. You could argue that we have taken over – I think there are around twelve establishments owned by stars of the show the last time I counted. The highlights include:

- **Amy Childs** opening a beauty salon and then a boutique – when she opened her shop, she said, 'We've got chandeliers in there and wallpaper with diamonds on it. I'd describe it as sparkly, classy and elegant, just like me.'

- **Harry's World** – which offers 'a variety of fantastic products including clothing, make-up, jewellery, bags and shoes'. Harry is a grafter, he works so hard and I have so much respect for him and his mum, Karen. They put so many hours into making Harry's World a success. He has a great eye for fashion and the shop always looks fantastic.

- **Lucy Meck** opened her boutique, but work pressure means that she isn't there as much as she could be and I think her *Results with Lucy* website and fitness programme take up a lot of her time now.

- **Joey** obviously opened up Fusey, though is rarely there.

- **Charlie** opened his deli, **Gemma** has her shop, **Danielle Armstrong** opened her boutique in Hornchurch, which is close to Brentford, **Lydia** has Bella Sorello and **Jess Wright** had With Love, Jessica – not forgetting the legendary **Sugar Hut**, the scene of many a drama in the show and still very much seen as 'the' place to go if you want to bump into the cast (or in the case of the boys, very much where you go if you want to pull a groupie!). Sugar Hut got so much attention in the early days, it is to blame for most of the *TOWIE* break-ups, as that is where the boys get themselves into trouble! I go to Sugar Hut quite often with my friends and the team from Minnies Boutique. Mick and his team there always look after us.

As far as eating goes, Essex is packed with great places for lovely food and drink. I genuinely think it is important to support local businesses, especially having one myself, and do all I can to tweet and be pictured out and about at local places I love. These include:

Tarantino

www.tarantinobrentwood.co.uk
60 Crown Street, Brentwood, Essex CM14 4BA

This lovely Italian place is a great place to go for any *TOWIE* fan. It is warm and cosy, the staff are lovely and the food is just like being in Italy. It has a casual and relaxed vibe and is perfect for a date. Sometimes they have live music, which is hilarious. I have filmed quite a lot of scenes here over the years but I still love coming here for a normal night out. They even do gluten-free pasta!

Alec's Restaurant

www.alecsrestaurant.co.uk
Navestock Side, Brentwood, Essex CM14 5SD

This is a bar and grill tucked away just outside Brentwood and a good place to go to get away from filming venues. The menu has a great selection and you are always really well looked after, they do an amazing soft-shelled crab starter and the surf and turf main course is delicious. Their desserts are pretty hard to resist too! I haven't been for a while as me and Joey would come here a lot, but now things are less raw I will definitely be going back soon.

Sheesh Restaurant

www.sheeshrestaurant.co.uk
Ye Olde King's Head, High Road, Chigwell, Essex IG7 6QA

This is a fun and lively restaurant that became a firm favourite with locals as soon as it opened up, and it is one of Billie's favourites. It does delicious Turkish food and has a great vibe – the perfect place to go with a large group to celebrate a birthday or a girls' night out. You have to be organized though – tables of four are often booked up three months in advance. Staff are lovely, portions are great value for money and it is noisy and buzzy. Quite a lot of the cast love it here and it is the venue of choice for a party or bigger group outing.

Welcome Inn Chinese Restaurant

49 High Street, Hornchurch, Essex RM11 1TP

I have been going to this lovely family-run restaurant for years now and I love it! It is tucked away at the quiet end of the high street and is calm and discreet, with tinted windows and a small dark green sign. You could almost miss it. There are classic round tables for large groups, though it would be tight for a massive party, as it is quite small inside. A Chinese is my biggest treat and the food here is always amazing. It is a combination of Szechuan and Peking cooking with the best Crispy Duck and Chicken Chow Mein. What I love most about this place is that everyone is a regular and for such a simple place, it has the best buzz. The food is delicious and the staff look after you so well, I recommend it to anyone who loves Chinese.

Smiths Restaurant, Ongar

Fyfield Road, Ongar, Essex CM5 0AL

This is an amazing fish restaurant in Ongar that I love going to for a special occasion. It has been going since 1958 and provides fresh and sustainable seafood. For me it is as good as Scotts in Mayfair or J Sheekey (in fact, that's where the head chef trained). It has the longest fish menu you can imagine and a selection of great wines to accompany every type. Inside it is so cosy – with a welcoming fire, exposed brickwork and a snug bar upstairs all tucked away, where you can watch delicious cocktails being mixed while you wait for your table. It is a proper grown-up place, no kids under twelve allowed, and big groups have to book in advance. It is definitely the perfect place for a treat meal out.

2

Building a Business

Minnies Boutique

Sometimes when I look around Minnies, I can't believe it is ours. It is every girl's dream to own a clothes shop, but, more importantly, what I love most about it is the fact that it is a family affair and we have all worked so hard to make sure we have a thriving business we are proud of. The biggest misconception about us starting the shop is that because we were on the show we must have had tons of money to invest from the start. That couldn't be further from the truth. Even when me and Billie were young Mum always had to work hard to make sure that we had what we needed – she was always on the go and never relied on a man to provide for her. She has always been a modern and independent woman and she is so proud she has passed that on to me and Billie, and I know she will pass it on to Nelly too. It has always been really important to me to provide for myself and so when the shop idea came up it seemed the perfect way for all us independent women to launch something new that we could enjoy as a family.

The idea came about just as Series 1 was coming to a close. A lot happened in that series in terms of our media profile – we were starting to be recognized out and about, we were in magazines a lot with positive comments on our style and people were really interested in where I was getting my outfits from. Amy and I were being inundated with requests to wear clothes by certain designers to promote on the show and at red carpet events, and, to my amazement, the things we were wearing were selling out right away. To be honest, it was becoming difficult to find something different to wear for both the show and out and about. I was permanently raiding Billie's wardrobe to mix things up a bit and driving her mad!

I remember really clearly sitting round Billie's kitchen table with my mum, Billie and my aunty Libby when we decided to open a boutique. When you are thinking about starting a business, it is rare that the first idea is the best idea or that someone else hasn't thought of it already – I mean, a clothes shop was hardly an Einstein moment never thought of before. But I also knew from the calls I got that there was a demand for decent clothes, at the right price, as seen on TV. It was a risk to throw money into something fairly early on in the *TOWIE* process when we weren't sure that it would last. (Billie wasn't even in the show at that point and I had no idea I would stay so long.) We watched all around us as more and more cast members opened up competitive shops, and we panicked, until we realized a simple thing. It wasn't the idea of a clothes shop that needed to be unique, we were the bit that needed to be unique. We knew how we were going to run it from day one and we knew it would remain central to everything we went on to do, and it has been. I think this is because we are hard-working by nature and want to be the best, but also we had family money invested and knew we had to do it right. The pressure was on from the start on that front and we couldn't let anyone down – not Mum, Aunty Libby or the fans. It was the start of a bigger idea for a business empire that went beyond *TOWIE* and that would benefit the whole family in the long run. I wanted to invest smart from the start so I wasn't tempted to waste my earnings.

It wasn't easy: we didn't have loads of money but we knew we wanted something for us that was separate from the show, something real that we could invest in and something that would keep us in the public eye if it all ended tomorrow. (I have never been under any illusions that it can all disappear just as quickly as it materialized – you see it every day with people far more famous than me.) We were all in agreement that we didn't want to get a loan from a bank so we decided to pool the money we had. Aunty Libby used some money from the recent sale of her house and I decided to increase the number of photo shoots and personal appearances I was booking.

I knew right from the start that I had to use my 'fame' wisely and build firm foundations quickly, so branching out with Minnies seemed like a sensible start on the business ladder. It still astonishes me how many of the cast haven't thought that way, how many don't have real lives running alongside the show and who still, all these years later, rely simply on being papped out and about and PAs to fund their lifestyles. Mario was great at the beginning, he had a proper job as a tailor, he was a hard worker and things were great between him and Lucy before she introduced him to the show. Then his head was turned and he let it all go. Mario loves the ladies and couldn't get over the girls who threw themselves at him. He turned his back on his old life, and his old morals. I really think he and Lucy could have been married by now if he had stayed making suits. Those boys still think they own Essex: they work out, pull girls, get involved in scandals, turn up at clubs and drink and whatever else to excess and spend their days sleeping it off. Or else they are like Joey and bring out ranges and open up shops, only to promote them a bit and forget all about them. I still can't get over the whole Fusey launch. Joey didn't have a clue what he was doing – I did all the decoration, sourced the stock, pulled it all together. I supported Joey out of love as I wanted him to have his own project and something to be proud of. I did as much as I could to make it a success for him. I had learned a lot from Minnies and being together meant of course I wanted to help him out and give him my experience.

Don't get me wrong, we were no business gurus when we opened Minnies, but at least we had the basics and we understood fully that a lot of our customers would be fans of the show coming to see us. We were determined to build our lives around the business as that's what would survive long after the show and well after people stopped asking for our autographs. We work there every single Saturday unless we have a filming commitment or a work thing that we can't reschedule. Other than that, we are there selling clothes and having photos taken, signing autographs, helping people try on outfits, as we know that's what is required. Even with the arrival of Nelly, Billie is doing as many shifts as she ever did, as well as combining it with working at Jam Kidswear, which is directly next door to Minnies. We're proud to put our heart and soul into the business and wouldn't have it any other way. We also know that we owe it to the fans to be present and involved. I think you can count on one hand the number of times Joey has actually been to Fusey since the big opening. He opened it and lost interest and that was that. It is the same for a lot of the cast and ex-cast. Others who put the graft in are Charlie Sims, he works full time at his deli and is determined to make a go of it and I really respect that. It is so nice to be able to see something of substance after all the hard work and there is nothing like a business that you can keep reinvesting in and expanding. And, as I mentioned earlier, Harry Derbidge is a great businessman and is really successful with his business and very hands-on each day. I think the key thing is to surround yourself with like-minded people you can trust to be hard-working and supportive, people who want to get out what they put in. It is worth remembering that you pay your own wages and there is no such thing as a sick day or hangover duvet day. If you don't open up, nobody will and me and Billie are very aware that our fame is a big draw for those who visit the shop, that's part of what we offer to the business and part of why it works. We also know that we have to look our best in order to promote the look and feel of the business. Even after the heaviest night out, I will get under the cold shower to wake myself up, put on my make-up and get to the shop for opening, there is no running away if you want to make money and having others rely on you is a great incentive.

Anyway, back to the opening of the shop. Using the PA money and some of my savings, I came up with my £5,000 share and we found the shop in Brentwood that we still have. Back then I remember I had just started to earn some good money and I remember chasing my manager Adam to find out when I would have £5,000 to put into the business pot, so we could move things along faster. There were some obvious things that needed addressing before any of us invested money at all – the first thing was to make sure our business plan was up to it. We had to be competitive – we asked ourselves, is there a market for what you want to do? If so, how big is that market? How will you find your customer? What is the competition? For us this was relatively simple given the attention our outfits got. I knew that designers wanted me to wear their clothes on the show as I was constantly sent things (as was Billie when she joined). That was the easy bit. We had to learn about fashion, how to put outfits together, what suited our shapes, what fabrics photographed well. Our business depended on the stock we picked and how we marketed it, of course it did. But at the beginning it depended on the idea that all the girls who tuned into *TOWIE* and bought the magazines we were in, wanted to dress like us and be like us. We were on the front line in the early days – if magazines didn't like what we were wearing, we wouldn't shift it in the shop and then we were in trouble. It was also about overall image – falling out of clubs and puffing away on cigarettes wasn't going to help our brand, so we had to think about who and what we associated ourselves with. Now things are different, I like to think we have built up brand trust and that customers know there's nothing stocked in Minnies we wouldn't all wear in a heartbeat. It has been interesting and, as time has gone on, the brand trust has grown and grown and that applies to Mum too. There's been loads of times she's been papped in something with me or Billie and the phone has rung off the hook trying to find out where it is from. It probably helps that she looks so young!

The other advice I was given was to ask – What's your USP? Ours was the free marketing Billie and me could offer and our presence in the shop, especially at the start. That was, and still is, the drill. We are proud that we were the first to come up with the idea and open a shop and get our business online. Obviously we set a trend, as others then began to pop up all over Brentwood and Essex, which is great.

It is fairly well documented how the shop began life – it was all tied in to the show, which meant dates kept moving around and lots of favours were pulled in. The truth was that it was a horrendous time for all of us. We were stressed out and bickering with each other about who had what job and it was all down to the producers and their completely unrealistic idea of what was possible when opening a new shop. We had been due to open officially in the fourth episode of Series 2, but then the producers brought the date forward by demanding it open in the first episode to launch the second series. Sheer panic is the only way to describe it – we were in there the night before until well after midnight, eating a Chinese takeaway on the floor, surrounded by clothes and packaging, stickering and steaming every garment. We pulled in every favour we possibly could – even the cash desk was free after we nabbed a big glittery bit of granite someone was throwing out! We knew what the fans would want – it had to be fairly OTT – so we went for pink and lots of leopard print. The idea was out and out glam. Billie often says that now she dreams of a nice white minimalist space – think Victoria Beckham – but we know we have to create the right environment for the clientele, so we keep it on the right side of kitsch and fun.

You have to learn so fast and react so quickly, especially with the online side of things, but the actual shop got off to an amazing start – bigger than any of us could have hoped or dreamed it would be. We really couldn't believe it. Everyone says it takes you a year to break even when you start up your own business; we broke even in the first month. We couldn't have been prouder. The big growth over the years has been online. Once Billie joined the show we were both on air in top-to-toe Minnies so it was like the shop getting advertising for free. It isn't just about clothes being on the show either. There was once a blue jumpsuit I was papped in just out and about in London. We sold out immediately – 130 of them. We reordered another forty and put them online at 9 a.m. The next day, by 10 a.m., they were sold out and that was just after a picture of me in the *Daily Mail*. We can be inundated with calls to the shop when people see us on the show wearing something specific – people are desperate to get their hands on it so we do try to keep the lines going, but we also like to give it some feel of exclusivity so we do end certain lines after one or two reorders. This creates a deliberate 'must-have' feel and gets people checking the site more often so they don't miss out.

It was strange to suddenly become walking advertisements for our family business, but, I won't lie, it has been tough working with family and there have been plenty of showdowns – never about money, we all trust each other completely, more disagreements about the division of labour. I think sometimes my aunty Libby, who is very much the 'numbers' person (the accounts, stock levels, etc.) and my mum (who is all over every detail, stocks the shop every night and even answers the phone!) can feel that Billie and I get the glamorous end of the bargain. After all, we have three offices and loads of staff that need managing, books that need balancing, buying appointments that need attending and all sorts of small details like online promotional codes that need deciding about, and often me and Billie just can't be there for certain decisions as we have photo shoots to attend for the website. I know it can seem like one long round of hair, make-up and dressing up, but those days are long. It is such a balancing act. In that sense, the shop comes first when it comes to our time; it is just time spent differently from the rest of the people who work there. That can be hard to explain sometimes and resentment does creep in – I remember telling Mum that we couldn't attend a particular financial sit-down, and being met with the rather sarcastic response: 'I'll just go on my own, shall I?' Can you imagine working with your family members? It is great at times but at other points it has caused problems and arguments – more than I think it would if we were just business partners in the standard way. But it is chicken and egg: the truth is that us being in the public eye is what helps the shop to be the success that it is and everyone involved knows and respects that. We do long photo shoots modelling the clothes and will then get photographed by the press in them – just one of those can be enough to send the website into meltdown and sell out a whole range and that is more than worth its weight in gold. Day to day, I am involved in the buying, meetings, stock ordering, social media, research, working in the store and attending events, if requested and linked into Minnies.

As I said, we had no business qualifications so we made mistakes. Billie still says now that she's picked up so many tips of what not to do and is putting it all to good use at the moment with her children's clothing business Jam Kidswear. We are proud of some very impressive statistics around the online launch – 410,000 hits in the first ten minutes, record selling out of items modelled by me and Billie and, when she is papped out and about, my mum, who looks good in everything.

The shop itself is great and always packed: we have school trips, hen dos that come all the way from Scotland, birthday trips with girls arriving in limos – you name it, they come to shop! The online business is the thing though. That's where you see the difference and where we are concentrating our efforts. It feels good to know that we have had three profitable years, and now, with our own ranges to add to the mix, it isn't just because me and Billie are wearing it that people are buying it. When people shop online it is because they genuinely love the clothes that we are sourcing and they like how the website works, and that is a huge achievement for me, a girl who left school at sixteen, to open a shop in the middle of a recession.

Obviously I am delighted that our business venture can be known as a success story, but most of all I am happy for our mum. Opening the shop has given her a new lease of life and I love seeing her so busy and in her element. She finally has something for herself – security, her own flat, her share in a thriving business. She's a nanny now, which brings her so much joy, and she is independent and loving life – she never stops telling me and Billie how proud she is of us and how much she loves us.

My mum is such an unbelievably strong woman who would do anything for her girls and has spent most of her life sacrificing herself for us. She has taught me and Billie to be loving and loyal, but, most of all, to take care of ourselves and strive for whatever we want. She's an amazing example – she had me at twenty-two and Billie is just eleven months older than me, so she was such a young mum, and it certainly wasn't an easy introduction to motherhood as she had to deal with our biological dad, Lee, who left when I was two years old. From what I gather, he was a seductive bad boy who made his money as a successful market trader. He did well and when we were really tiny we all lived on an eighteen-acre farm in Upminster. But money trouble hit and his drinking got out of control. Added to that was the drug use – he was taking speed and it made him volatile and awful to live with. Mum always says that the violence was the hardest thing, never knowing what was coming or what would set him off, and then there is the general unpredictability that comes with those who take drugs. Mum finally left, and her family were amazing and made sure that the three of us were safe. Luckily for us, we stayed close to Dad's parents – we love our Nanny Wendy, and she was always there for us, and we still see her all the time. Mum never stopped us from seeing our biological dad, if that was what we wanted, and Nanny Wendy used to take us and did all she could to help us stay close to him. But it didn't last. We had no time for the man who had half strangled our mum and who beat her up so badly she had to go to hospital and tell lie after lie about how she got the injuries. His idea of trying to put things right was doing a story with the *Daily Star* when I was in the *Celebrity Big Brother* house and gravely ill. They ran with the headline: 'Estranged ex-druggie father of Sam Faiers begs her for another chance'.

It didn't work and, as far as me and Billie are concerned, our real dad is Dave. He has been in my life since I was two and we love him as much as if he were our biological dad. But things haven't been easy for him and my mum either. It is well documented that he has been in prison for various things over the years and has been separated from us whilst he served that time. Things were tricky when I was younger. At one time he was away for eight years, which was incredibly tough on us all. We even had to spend five years in Spain sort of hiding out with him, you could say 'absconding', and his difficulties have meant that Mum has had to spend a lot of time on her own and fend for herself without a partner by her side as he saw out his sentences and paid for his crimes. We suffered by not having him there and by being uprooted to live abroad but we are still all close as a family and love and look out for each other.

I don't know what will happen now he is out. It's great to have him about and he adores Nelly like we all do, being a granddad has been great for him. I hope he gets his happy ending. When Nelly was born it gave my dad a new lease of life. He has his own construction business now and is really enjoying family life and work. It is really hard for him: he's been away from us and, rightly or wrongly, life goes on. My mum has grown and changed and become used to being alone, while Billie has had Nelly and I have had my fair share of medical and romantic drama. There's a lot of time to make up, but we will. We love him and will do all we can to support him – we were there for the trial and wrote letters of support to show the judge how much he meant to us and how we all wanted to help him get back on his feet. Whatever happens, he will always be our dad.

Build your Business

Make the dream come true. I feel very proud of the business that we have created outside of the show. It has a made profit from day one, is well run, reasonably priced and we all work very hard. We have had ups and downs, but I would do it all again in a heartbeat. It has been one of the best experiences to have come out of the show. Now, I know I am no Alan Sugar, but here are some tips for getting started on *your* business dream:

- Be realistic about your own circumstances. Don't quit your regular salary until you have your business plan firmly in place and up and running. It is a bit like me staying in *TOWIE* whilst doing all the other business-related things I did. Make sure the time is right before you jump and that there is a net to catch you.

- 'Think big and dream big, right from day one,' says Sheryl Sandberg and she's right – remember that everyone has to start somewhere but that there isn't any point if you don't aim high. Always aim for growth and scaling up your business. For example, we knew once the Brentwood shop made a profit month after month that it was then time to try something new. We decided to take the brand to customers up north with the pop-up shop idea and then, most recently, the shop in Beverley. But that was

44

only when we had a total handle on the original shop, when the brand was cemented and when we knew the appetite was wider than the Essex border. We had lots of offers for expansion but they never felt right at the time.

- It isn't easy and anyone who says that it is clearly isn't doing it right. If you work for yourself you've got to be the best boss you've ever had and practise what you preach. Unpack the boxes and ticket the stock along with Saturday girls, clean the shelves and mirrors and hoover the changing rooms. If you don't care about your business, why should others?

- We were lucky that we made money from day one, and that's carried on. But we were warned that lots of small businesses lose money in the first couple of years. So make sure you have a back-up fund. Be realistic – do you have enough cash to live on if things don't grow and expand as fast as you'd like?

- Keep overheads small – although we have grown massively, we still only have the staff we need rather than the number that would make our lives really easy. Our Beverley shop has one full-time staff member in the week and four at the weekend for when school is out and we expect the younger shoppers. Me and Billie are still counted as 'staff' and are expected to pull our weight accordingly.

- Expand all in good time and make sure the structure can cope with the growth plan that you set yourself. This is one reason that we still stock a certain amount of brands successfully, and in moderation, rather than branching out into stocking our own line. We want to own the market consistently and successfully for a good while before we expand into our own ranges.

- You need to be hungry – motivation to succeed is key and will keep you going, you need loads of drive. You also need to never be too big for your boots – we still answer the phone and label up the stock with the rest of the staff in the shop. There are jobs that need doing and we all muck in. I like to think we lead by example. We have made lots of costly mistakes, but you learn from them and then don't make them again.

- Know your brand and walk the walk – me and Billie are proud to be so hands-on in the shop. You can't inspire people if you fake it.

- Customer service is key. We take great pride in the fact that we have always had amazing customer service. When a customer comes into the shop we expect our staff to greet them and talk to them so that the cusomer enjoys the Minnies experience from start to finish.

- Have the right people in place – we all have strengths that we should work towards and we can't be good at everything.

3
Gossip and Drama

After being in the show from the very beginning, I know more than anyone that there are a lot of divas around and that loyalty isn't a given, but even I was surprised by how badly I was treated over my departure from the show. After all that commitment and all those episodes, I was given just two minutes to say my goodbyes. I wouldn't have minded so much if the producers hadn't gone to the trouble of talking through how my exit would go and agreeing that I could make it fairly emotionally charged. I was gutted. I'd thought out and filmed the scene where I'd talked about the other cast members and my time on the show and they didn't use any of it. I had things I wanted to say but they binned the lot.

I had a very clear idea of how it should be, not least as a thank you to the loyal fans who had been with me since the very first episode. But when it came to it, they axed it all – I guess that's just the way it goes. What mattered most was that Billie was there with me. We both got a bit emotional really at the thought of not being on screen together any more. I had a whole big thing planned but I should have known things would be taken out of my hands when the producers asked me in advance if I would mind sharing the scene with Ferne. I wanted to have Billie and the other people who had been on the *TOWIE* journey with me from day one. I felt they had been along for the ride with me and that it would be special to have them there. I wanted it to be a celebration of me and the few members of the old-school cast who were left, and for the viewers to know that I didn't think I was too big for the show. I know the producers wanted to leave the door open.

I still watch the show and I do get pangs when I watch certain episodes – especially when I see Billie, and now Nelly, on it – but there are lots of things I will not miss. Although one of the deciding factors in leaving was to try to give me and Joey the best chance to make things work – truth is that I had come to the end of feeling comfortable on the show. I guess I grew up on it and there comes a time when you naturally outgrow your surroundings. I will always have the show to thank for the amazing opportunities that have come my way. I know it was a brilliant launch pad for me and I am so glad I didn't make the same mistake as others had done and walk away from it before I was established. A few people thought they were bigger than the show before they were ready to fly the nest. If you think of all those who have left, the only ones to really take off have been Joey and Mark Wright (though Mark's has mostly been down to *Strictly Come Dancing*. Getting engaged to Michelle Keegan hasn't done his profile any harm either!).

The question I am most often asked is, 'Is the show scripted or is it real?' The answer is, at the beginning it was real but now it feels more like a soap, which was another reason it felt like a good time to be getting out. I found it increasingly hard to live my life with a potential storyline in mind and for some of the cast it dictates everything in a really unhealthy way. For example, I don't think Lydia and Arg would have got back together if Lydia hadn't had to go back to the show because there weren't that many opportunities for her outside it. Her vintage clothing line didn't really take off and I know she tried a few other things that didn't quite work out. Would Joey's cousin and Mario have got it together and done all those press interviews about being a 'couple' if they didn't both need it? Certainly on-screen drama makes for more airtime and that equals more publicity off screen. It also makes me wonder how genuine Joey's cousin was about Elliott Wright or if it was just time for another on-screen love interest for maximum airtime. You by default tend to gravitate to people on the show; we've all been guilty of doing it!

It is really hard not to let it change your personality – you can see it with some of the couples where there is one of them fighting to be the person who does the dumping. Or where the fame goes to their heads and means that bad behaviour becomes the norm, like when Mario repeatedly cheated on Lucy because he 'couldn't help himself' when girls apparently threw themselves at him in a way that made it impossible for him to resist. It is like living in a weird no-man's-land where things don't quite seem real and where it is easy not to have a firm grip on the world and easy to make excuses for bad behaviour. That's where it can feel like double standards in Essex. The men are allowed to get drunk, let girls 'innocently' sleep in their beds, get with people they shouldn't. But if the girls do it, that's a whole different ball game and the boys feel they can all get together and pass judgement. I do think the girls should have respect for themselves – I can't count the amount of girls I see letting themselves down when I'm on a night out in Essex. It is like they think the boys from the show are the answer to their prayers – they want to be famous at any cost, even if it means acting like total idiots! Some girls go on TV shows like *The X Factor* or *Take Me Out* so they can hit the headlines, and some sleep with the likes of Mario, Lewis or Ricky. *TOWIE* boys really aren't worth it, though they act like sex gods around the place! All the wrong kind of female attention gives them a false impression of themselves and means they spend their time punching above their weight and full of themselves. Arg truly believes that it is his right to pull leggy models and is always after the hottest girl in the bar!

That said, boys should have respect – don't treat girls badly or just like objects. Remember how you were brought up and imagine if it was your sister being treated badly by someone like you, I'm sure it would be a different story then.

Certainly things have changed since the beginning of the show – to me it was definitely much more innocent and far less cynical back then. I think that explains why the bond between the hard-core originals is so strong. I mean, take Gemma Collins for instance, she rubs so many people up the wrong way but me and Billie, we love her! A lot of people don't warm to her – mainly because she is so volatile. The thing about Gemma is that she is in such a different place from the rest of us – she is thirty-three and has been so unlucky in love and all she wants is to find a good man to settle down and have babies with. Of the blokes who have had the biggest impact on her and her time in the show, I think Rami has the most to answer for. He dented her confidence so badly – Gemma has a very soft centre behind all the bluster – you only have to have seen her on *I'm a Celebrity . . . Get Me Out of Here!* to work that out. She is full of insecurities. Out of us all, she's the one I really want to find a 'happy ever after'. The situation with Arg doesn't help – there's no doubt that she loved him deeply, and he knows it! I think he can be guilty of toying with her emotions a bit – he knows that she would have him back in a heartbeat. I felt so sorry for her when Lydia came back to the show; you could see she was distraught. I think out of everyone she has dated and fallen in love with, in her eyes, he's the one she can properly imagine making a life with – they do have a lot in common and I think he is the one bloke she doesn't feel so self-conscious around. Perhaps that's because behind the 'cheeky chap' banter, Arg knows what it is like to have body issues – he is always trying to lose weight and knows that, up against blokes like Dan and Elliott, he isn't exactly torso of the year!

But Arg is his own worst enemy. He has been in the show from the start and, unlike the rest of us, he doesn't have anything to show for it financially. He lacks any kind of get-up-and-go – he's a bit of a slob really and that's nothing I haven't said to his face! He got a flat from Mark Wright senior and then didn't bother moving into it for months on end. He can't even drive, cook, clean or iron, but, most importantly from a professional point of view, he is late for everything. When I was on the show, Arg was the one we all spent time waiting for before we could start filming and when he did turn up he was hungover and in no fit state to work. Arg went to rehab last year and from what I have heard the experience did him the world of good. All that said, I love Arg and he knows how much I do genuinely adore him. Despite all his shit-stirring (and, boy, he loves to stir things up by gossiping about others behind their backs! You can always rely on Arg to pass on a rumour, even before he knows if it is true!), he has a heart of gold and would do anything for anyone. He is a real softy underneath it all and I know he would love to settle down (although there will always be a part of him that genuinely thinks he has it in him to pull a supermodel, talk about self-confidence!). He's really slimmed down recently and looked great when I saw him.

To be fair, that is something all the boys share, the idea that fame means they can pull any girl they want – people like Kirk and Mario from the old camp were particularly like that. If you watch the first few series, their self-confidence is astonishing really! But the show was also a big new thing and why wouldn't good-looking boys take advantage when girls were keen to get with them? I don't blame them really. Since it started though, there have been other similar shows like

Made in Chelsea and there are lots more cute boys around so our boys have lots more competition!

There has definitely been a shift in the show in terms of the type of characters the producers are getting on board now. It seemed before that they used to concentrate on people who the viewers would like and want to see do well, family-friendly characters who induced affection – so even when Mario cheated, people still wanted him and Lucy to work it out and get their 'happy ever after', mainly because they remembered he could be decent but had just let fame turn his head. Now it seems that aggro-induced storylines are higher up the list of priorities. Viewers used to genuinely care what happened in the lives of the people on screen – characters like Amy and Harry used to be celebrated for their comedy chat and naive ways. It was light entertainment. Sometimes I tune in now and I can't keep up with who is slagging off who, who is cheating on who, who is manufacturing aggro to get storylines. But I am the show's biggest fan despite what any-one says. I still watch religiously and love seeing Billie, Nelly and my friends on there doing their thing. The show will always have a special place in my heart.

I think it is most noticeable too when old characters think about going back and see how much it has all changed. Take Harry Derbidge for example, he went back in Series 13 as Bobby-Cole Norris's boyfriend. He and Bobby had been see-ing each other for a few months and doing well, when it was suggested he go back in the show. Obviously Harry knew the drill, that they would look for the most dramatic storylines, but he didn't expect it to go as it did for him. Suddenly he was a 'cheat' (even though he'd been single when he'd slept with his ex). I heard on the Essex grapevine that Bobby was colluding with the producers and then stitching Harry up on screen for guaranteed airtime and Gemma was being encouraged to get herself right in the middle in order to cause maximum drama. She's admitted it was all manipulated. It also paved the way for Harry and Gemma's mums to enter the series – which is a trick I think producers had stolen from *Made in Chelsea* and the success of Binky Felstead's mum, Mummy Felstead. Don't get me wrong, I love it when all the mummies make the odd appearance, I think it is good to show where we all come from and how we were brought up, it is nice for our mums too, but this just involved a lot of shouting and slagging off. All in all it was a difficult storyline, not least as the fans didn't want to see Harry in those situations. They wanted the old Harry, who came out with the one-liners, who got dressed up in girls' clothes and had beauty treatments, the vulnerable Harry who did daft things but always had a good heart. In my opinion the mistake the producers made was that they tried to make him like the new lot, and it didn't work. It brought out the worst in Bobby too, who I thought started to look vicious and a bit desperate if you ask me. I think Harry made the right call not to let the storyline carry on. It was such a shame as it could have really worked, having a much-loved face from the start back on the screen, but I guess it just showed what a different place *TOWIE* was now.

For me, the roots of the show's success will always hinge on the viewers wanting what is best for the characters they love – in my opinion they don't care about Lewis and Grace not getting together, Jasmin and Dan not going on a date, Lockie maybe cheating on Danielle. They don't want the boys behaving like animals and cheating on lovely girls like Lydia, Jess and Lucy by sleeping with fame-hungry Twitter stalkers. They want to see Arg wooing Lydia. They love Nanny Pat, Carol and Debbie dishing out wise and motherly advice to Ricky, Arg and Mario. And they want to see Jess find a real man not a boy like Ricky and they want Gemma to meet 'the one'. I am not sure that can happen when they keep bringing in new people all the time who seem to do nothing but cause trouble. The truth is that the show is unrecognizable from the one I joined and it was definitely the right time to move on when I did. For me it felt right and I had done my time and given all I could give.

Ways to keep it real and survive living in Essex

- Don't get sucked in to other people's jealousy and bad vibes. Concentrate on you and what makes you happy, not what lies others choose to tell about you to hide their own dark behaviour.

- You can't please all of the people all of the time, so don't try. You know who matters to you so stick with them and stop worrying about what others think of you.

- There's a lot to be said for going on a life detox, a bit of time on your sofa with a box set and your own company can inject some reality back into your life. Surround yourself with people you know love and respect you.

- Do your job and go home. Try and separate home from work – easier said than done in my case as I lived my life on a show watched by thousands of people – but it is important to switch off. If you listened to gossip all the time you'd never trust a soul.

- Try not to be swayed by others. I am a great believer in taking as you find, if someone hasn't done you wrong then stand by them until they prove you wrong. Always give someone the benefit of the doubt.

- The truth will always out – never forget you will be found out. Especially if you misbehave on your own doorstep! And especially in Essex!

4

Me and Joey

Me and Joey. Oh god, where to start? The drama!! To be honest, we could start pretty near the end, with my illness. As Kelly Clarkson says, 'What doesn't kill you makes you stronger' and all that. But in Joey's case, I think me getting ill made him realize he still had feelings for me. It is obvious that, as you read this, things didn't work out between us, and that was definitely the last time we will be giving it a try. I could go into the ins and outs of why we finally split. There is certainly plenty that would cause people to re-evaluate their perception of 'poor Joey' and plenty that isn't true in his book, but the truth is it's not worth going into – it didn't work out and we are better off apart. That said, there is a part of me that wishes he hadn't been back in touch after my exit from the *Celebrity Big Brother* house – I could have saved myself a lot of heartache and wasted time.

I do still sit here and wonder why he got back in contact with me, especially given how it ended the last time. Looking back, it was always dysfunctional. I just couldn't see it then as I was in love and sometimes you just have that connection with someone that overrides everything, including common sense.

We were young and naive at the start, but there was no denying the attraction as soon as we met. We had known each other for a while before he appeared on *TOWIE*. Essex is such an incestuous place and Joey was friends with one of my ex-boyfriends from when I was younger. I'd seen him around town, at parties and clubs. We knew each other to say hi to and his cousin, Charlie, had just started seeing my friend Ferne. We didn't really start getting chatty until after Series 1 and one particular night was when it all kicked off. I went to London on a girlie night out with Ferne to Revolution. Me and Joey had some banter and he got my number. Nothing really happened as he had just split from a girlfriend at the time. The paps were out in force and, for a joke, I suggested we go out and get our picture taken and that he could be my 'mystery man'. We went outside and they got their shots and I got in the car and said goodbye. Then, out of the blue, Joey stuck his head through the open window of my car and kissed me! It made the papers and magazines and the rest is sort of history. The *TOWIE* producers loved the pap shots and instantly fell in love with his personality and banter and knew the viewers would too. There is no doubt that Joey has bags of charisma and that thing that makes women just want to love and look after him. He is also very, very funny. He was a hit all round. Joey and his girlfriend had already split up, and he and I got together and went out for four months the first time, despite our first date involving me being taken to the rubbish dump!

I am quite well known for being old-fashioned when it comes to men and dating. I do, despite the stick I get, believe in men offering to pay for the first few dates and refusing to let you go halves. It isn't to do with the money at all, I am a very financially independent girl, I just think it makes a really good impression and shows he is keen and I like that. I never want a really flash first date (things with Joey would never have got off the ground if I did, given his venue choice!). But I am such a romantic at heart, I love it when thought and planning has gone into things – if the bloke has taken the time to find out what I like doing, or he has asked the advice of Billie or a close friend. A favourite restaurant, candles, picking me up from home, pulling out my chair for me – they are all ways to my heart. I love manners in a man. I also knew that the rules were slightly different for me, everyone told me, 'Keep your wits about you'. The downside of me being in the public eye is that I can attract the wrong kind of intentions from some blokes. You do have to be a bit more careful who you trust and know they are genuine in wanting to go out with you. Sometimes it can be just about headlines and attracting attention, if they need help with their career (it is similar to your so-called 'friends' who speak out to newspapers and magazines). Mums are good for spotting that!

In all honesty, our relationship the first time round never really got off the ground, I think the pressure to be the 'new couple' was there right from the start. Plus, looking back, it seems clear to me that Joey didn't like me going out and being myself – I am a party girl, I love socializing, seeing my friends and letting my hair down. I work hard, I don't get into trouble, I just love to unwind with my family and friends, have a few drinks and dance. But Joey never saw that – it was very much one rule for him and another for me. He would so often go out with the lads. Joey was doing PAs four times a week on average, so whether it was work or play he was in a club. It never bothered me. We were both young and deserved to cut loose now and again.

It first started to come to a head after the end of Series 2 when we went on holiday to Marbella with our mates, even though we were a couple. It was a new relationship. I was going on a girls' holiday and then Joey decided to come out with his boys, as he was so in love with me. I was already having doubts at that point – Joey was just so young and needy and didn't seem to understand that we could do our own thing and still be very much together. It was all too suffocating too soon. I was there with my girls to let my hair down but it seemed to be one drama after another with Joey – he didn't like the attention he was getting around the resort, and it didn't help that he got robbed whilst he was there, which was awful for him. They took everything including his Louis Vuitton suitcase and £4,000.

It was inevitable that things would start to go wrong given how hectic it was for both of us with the show. I think we both got carried away with everything and didn't invest any time in being together. We are both very hard-working people – unlike some on the show – and we both knew it could all end any minute (we had no idea we would stay in the show for as long as we did) and we wanted to make sure that we didn't waste a minute. Around Series 2 and 3, *TOWIE* just kept getting more and more popular – the ratings went up and we were getting a lot more tabloid coverage too. Suddenly the weekly mags like *Now* and *Reveal* were full of wall-to-wall *TOWIE* pictures, captions, interviews and made-up stories from 'close sources'. Joey was doing PAs all the time – practically every night of the week – and I was with Billie and Mum sorting out Minnies and doing my own appearances to earn some money. The shop was really starting to take off – we had our online site that needed redesigning and me and Billie were always finding stock and doing what we could around filming schedules. We believed in being properly hands-on and would happily pick and pack ourselves (I love that job, it is very therapeutic!) and work in the shop as often as we could. We still do and Nelly comes too now. We didn't want it to be like when others have opened up shops, that it is just another thing to try like a calendar or another endorsement. We were determined it wouldn't fail. But it was a downer on me and Joey – we were busy, grumpy, tired and snappy, and I hated that I'd become the moaning girlfriend having a go at him for getting in so late and never having time for me. Something had to give and it was me and Joey.

He took it really badly when I finished with him shortly after the ill-fated holiday to Marbs. To be honest, even when we got back together and he proposed, he was still bringing it up then. He didn't ever let it drop. As usual, he ran to his nearest and dearest and they all agreed what a terrible person I was to hurt him like that. I was working in Manchester. Even then there was the hint of paranoia that was hard to ignore further down the line, he was obsessed with the idea of me cheating even though I never gave him a single moment of worry. Somehow it was always me hurting him, like I was in the relationship with myself. I tried to be gentle – after all we both knew it had been a while coming and neither one of us was happy – but still it was easier to paint me as the bad one. You only have to read his book to see that.

Romantically my head was all over the place and I started seeing TJ again – despite having finished with him previously. It felt like there was unfinished business, so we decided to give it another shot just as Series 3 went on air. Inevitably, having seen how I worked on screen when I was in a relationship with someone, soon the producers started pushing for him to join the show – it was always much more exciting when there were couples dramas. We talked it through and, although it would have been a great opportunity, TJ decided he valued his privacy too much and he really didn't want to. That suited me after what had happened with me and Joey – there is just too much pressure. It is also what Billie and Greg have done with their relationship – apart from the big 'couple' moments like their engagement and the baby shower, Greg prefers to leave the limelight to Billie and it just works like that. Don't get me wrong, he supports her when it is all about their little family with Nelly – he is such a proud daddy and fiancé – but he likes Billie to be the one on the front line with the PR and he has his own career that is doing brilliantly.

In the end, TJ's wish for privacy turned out not to be an issue as things fizzled out and I found myself attracted to other 'unfinished business' in the shape of Mr Mark Wright. But, in reality, it didn't take long for me to remember that the only person Mark Wright could think about for longer than ten seconds was Mark Wright. He's a decent guy deep down but he was a player and not someone I could trust. He wanted it all on his own terms and I'm just not the sort of girl who drops everything to please a man. Luckily he seems settled with Michelle Keegan – she seems to be a good match for him and won't put up with any nonsense! We don't speak any more, which is a shame, but I wish him well. I think he has distanced himself from every aspect of his past life and that obviously includes exes, even though there was no drama, and he doesn't talk to Billie either. He is a good guy from a lovely family and I loved watching him on *Strictly Come Dancing* – believe me, having seen him in nightclubs growing up, I always knew he was a novice!

You probably get the sense that I don't like unfinished business, and where me and Joey are concerned, that's always how it has felt whenever we've split up. There's a weird connection, a push–pull that we can't control. But the first time we did split, it seemed for keeps, and I dated and worked hard, but always with him in the back of my mind. In fact, he was very much on my mind when I was on a trip to Dubai some time afterwards, and some old family friends who were with us asked me to call him as they were fans of his. He was back home, but he picked up and we chatted like old times. A few weeks later we were both at the TRIC Awards on the same table but not next to each other. We both tried to play it cool, but as the evening went on and we drank more, we were slowly edging round the table to be nearer and by the end of the night we had a kiss and a cuddle and that old spark was there for both of us, so we picked up where we had left off.

But really we had the same old problems and so much pressure was put on us by the producers of the show and by his family, and, to be honest, it didn't help that he ran to them every time we had an argument so that I was made out to be the bitch. The tabloids always said I was the one who 'wore the trousers' and there was a lot of sympathy for 'poor Joey'. We both agreed later that we let too many people have an opinion and got caught up in drama and gossip, which meant we both drank too much and rowed all the time. The difference is that I always understood this was part and parcel of normal life. Admittedly we did go through phases where we rowed non-stop and they were pretty explosive, but still, I have always been of the opinion that clearing the air is a good and healthy thing. But Joey had a real skill for twisting things round to suit him and playing on the 'little boy lost' act. Because he has never really been made to grow up and take responsibility for himself, he is incapable of accepting his part in anything and this was most obvious when the infamous 'Dubai Slap' almost ended up ruining my reputation and career.

We had decided to spend some quality time together and so had gone away to get some sun and relax – I love Dubai and it felt like the perfect place for us to recharge from filming and chill. We had been going through a particularly tough period of bickering and I really wanted us to make an effort with each other, away from the cameras in our real life. However, we did that classic thing of getting over-excited – we drank on the flight and got headachy and dehydrated. It was a day flight, so by the time we landed, we decided to go back to the hotel, shower and change and go to a club to get back on it.

We decided to go to a club with Chloe's on–off boyfriend who lives in Dubai and knows all the local sights and great places to hang out. It was a full-on night – we had a private table, the drinks kept coming, there were dancers everywhere and it was very easy to get carried away. We all got very drunk very quickly and, in classic style, me and Joey started to row. It got really late and I'd had enough. I had hit my wall and just wanted to get into bed. We had another row as Joey wanted to stay on and kept trying to persuade me – he was really going for it, but I wanted to go home. After all, we had come away to spend time together yet he was intent on getting wasted, and I was knackered and wanted to be fresh for the morning and enjoy the pool and sunshine, not be lying on a sunlounger with a banging head feeling all miserable.

So I left and went to find a taxi. I decided to drunkenly call Chloe and tell her about my evening and the fact that her boyfriend was there. I told her it had been quite an OTT night and that they were staying to carry on getting pissed. I remember the call well as she scared me a bit by saying that I should go back into the club and wait for them, that it was too dangerous to be on my own on the street when I'd had too much to drink. But I was fine – the service in Dubai is amazing and I soon had a cab and was safely back at our hotel. I took my clothes off (though I was too drunk to bother removing my make-up!) and passed out.

The next thing I knew it was the early hours of the morning and there was a huge commotion in our suite. Despite being at the club for hours and getting wasted, Joey had decided he didn't want to call it a night just yet and brought two blokes back for an 'after-party' in our bedroom. Not content with making loads of noise in the main bit of the room, they came over to the bed where I was sleeping and started pulling at the duvet, sort of mucking around, but because everyone was so drunk the tugging was quite vigorous. Even if I hadn't been sleeping and already starting to feel hungover, I wouldn't have found it remotely funny as I was naked underneath. There's me, Joey and two random blokes in a hotel room, me with no clothes on and everyone completely intoxicated. I woke up and felt very vulnerable and angry at Joey for putting me in this situation – bringing strangers back whilst I was in bed was not okay in my book and I just wanted them out.

As Joey was pulling at the bedclothes, I flung my hand over to the corner of the duvet in order to grab it and stop him showing two strange men everything that was under the covers. As I stretched my hand out and grabbed wildly at the air, my promise ring struck his face, completely by accident. I was screaming at him – 'Get out, get the hell out! What is wrong with you?' – and in anger got his phone and threw it at the wall, and we both watched it smash into pieces. I could see that it had scared him as his eyes went all big. I didn't see a mark on his face but after the initial shock of our row had worn off he just took the others over to the other side of the room and carried on drinking, albeit more quietly, until the sun came up.

The next day I was still fuming at him – I couldn't believe that he had brought men into our room and thought it would be funny to tug the covers off me. It is not acceptable to any girl in any situation to do that. I don't know what he was thinking or where his head was to do that.

He was in an awful shape, so hungover, still passed out on his side of the bed, the covers over his face. I was determined not to waste our first day in the hot sunshine, so I left him to sleep it off and went down to the pool.

Joey woke up and obviously worked out what had happened from the tiny cut near his eye and how awful he was feeling, but rather than come down and smooth things over, the Joey spin machine went into overdrive. He came down to the pool crying, gulping air in a really melodramatic way and shouting: 'What have you done to me? I'm bleeding. You hit me and then you left me to wake up on my own. You haven't even said sorry.' What was strange was that he kept taking pictures on his phone for evidence and sending them on to his cousin.

Of course, any kind of violence is unforgivable, whether it is dealt out by a man or a woman. It isn't ever okay to hit someone. Ever. If anyone knows that, it is me, after all that my mum had to put up with when it came to my dad and his beatings. I have watched her be strong and independent and put her life back together and she always told me and Billie, 'If a man ever hits you, you leave, no second chances.' It is the one thing we have both always known is non-negotiable in a relationship. I know it is the most destructive thing in the world. So of course I apologized. I would never have hurt Joey intentionally, ever, and I would never hit anyone. I tried to remind him what had happened – the drinks, the 'after-party' in our suite with me naked trying to sleep. I don't think it was acceptable to carry on like that, to bring strangers into my room is not a good move at any time. I was vulnerable and he was too drunk to be in control of the situation and how on earth he would have reacted if that story had been recounted back to him by me and he hadn't been there. He would have gone mental and questioned why I hadn't done something to get myself out of the situation or at least pre-serve my modesty. Finally I reminded him that we had both been drunk and that things had happened when we were both out of control, that it had happened when I tried to grab the duvet and I hadn't meant to hit him.

But no, that wasn't enough for Joey – the tears carried on, he phoned his cousin, sobbing down the phone that I'd slapped him and he couldn't show his face outside as it looked so awful. Despite the tiny scratch and regrettable black eye and his part in everything, there was no doubting who the villain was here, and yet again our relationship wasn't just for us, Joey had to share it with anyone who would listen. But this was a new low, accusing me of domestic violence and implying he was scared of me. We carried on the rest of the holiday and tried to move on but the 'incident' followed me around for ages and, in Series 9, it all came to a head.

His cousin couldn't resist getting herself involved in the drama back home, something she did yet again in Series 12 and 13 with Charlie and Ferne. There were barbed comments on screen, as Joey continued to play the put-upon boyfriend by relaying every cross word we'd had, crying to the boys but never, of course, admitting or really explaining his part in anything. As Billie said: 'What is it with your relationship? It's you, him and his cousin. Why?'

Joey's cousin became like a broken record about me, both on screen and in the press to promote the show, with her saying, 'If only people knew the truth about her, then they would know why I can't stand her'. Her favourite put-down was, 'People will find out soon what's what and then they will see her for what she is'. She insinuated pretty much everything, including that I'd had an affair. I felt I had no choice but to address it on the show – the viewers were getting totally the wrong idea from Joey's cousin's cryptic comments without having any context – I could have been a mass murderer for all they knew! That became clear when she came to my house to do a scene, despite promising Joey that she wouldn't say anything on screen as he didn't want her to. By that point, Frankie and Joey's cousin had hardly spoken to me for weeks and being on set waiting around for filming was such a strain, it was so uncomfortable. Joey's cousin (or the producers, I'm not sure who it was really) decided that we needed to clear the air. So instead she came round to have it out with me about my 'aggression' and we both ended up talking about what happened in Dubai without actually addressing it properly in a way that made any sense on screen. She was at pains to reinforce that she knew far more about mine and Joey's relationship than perhaps I was aware of. She went on about how hard it was to see him 'suffering', crying and devastated by our rows. I tried to put my point across – that it did take two to tango and that I would sit and listen to him on the phone recounting our rows and think, 'Why is he twisting it all round so much?' It was like the main aim was always to get the most sympathy, even if it meant re-writing history and telling lies. It was such an awkward scene, mostly because it didn't make any sense out of context and made it look like I had something dreadful to hide. It also didn't really give me the chance to emphasize that there are always two sides to every story, especially as I had told Joey so many times that we needed to keep our arguments just to us.

So I decided to take control of my situation for once, rather than letting others have the final word on my business, and I headed off all the rumours at the spa day with Billie and

Ferne. It was just after me and Joey had split again and the gossip machine was in overdrive. As far as Joey's family were concerned, it was a case of 'horrible hard-faced bitch Sam'. We sat by the indoor pool discussing how we were sure my ears would be burning as the whole of Essex discussed our recent break-up and I told them people could say what they liked but I knew that the only awful thing I'd ever done in our relationship was slap Joey once, but stupidly I used the unfortunate words: 'Everyone slaps their boyfriend'. Instantly I realized this was going to open a can of worms. I hadn't meant for it to come out the way it did and it was something I would later regret.

Everyone went into overdrive, and I understand it from the outside. As I said, I would never condone or inflict violence. I am not proud of what I did but I also know the full story and Joey isn't blameless and not once did he attempt to put the truth out there. Suddenly domestic violence charities came down on me like a ton of bricks. This went on for weeks – I was a 'thug', a 'disgusting human being' and an embarrassment to feminism. I lost a massive branding and endorsement deal, whilst others hung in the balance. It was a truly awful time – in fact, other than when Joey was in the jungle, it was the worst time in my career (but more of that later). As the storm rumbled on, not once did Joey come forward to give the real version of events and explain what really happened. Truth be told, there was a big part of me that thought he let it carry on, as he loved all the attention.

How to make a date into a relationship

- Remember to be emotionally available – don't let a previous disaster harden your heart. You have to be open to a first date becoming something more, even if it feels like early days. Be in the moment and you might be surprised.

- BUT, be sparing with your second chances – if he is messing you around at the start or doing things you don't like, it will only get worse once the honeymoon phase has worn off. The start should be intoxicating, not full of petty rows or games.

- Don't waste your time, know the warning signs early on and don't give him too much slack. He has to want to work hard for you and then know what to do to keep you.

- Keep things simple. The ultimate early dating no-no is the text game, if you have to wait more than a day for him to reply, make or confirm plans, then bin him. He's either seeing more than one girl, or he's keener to go out with the lads rather than you. Either way, he isn't worth your time. If he can't get the rules right at the start, he never will.

- Don't be the 'one before the one'. If you aren't sure about him or he won't commit, don't invest all your time and effort making him the perfect boyfriend. It is more than likely that he will take all your hard work to his next girlfriend and end up settling down with her!

- Don't pretend to like things you don't – if you go to one football match you will have to go to them all!

- Keep your identity. The early phase is a delicate balancing act of showing an interest in him and being intriguing, but be yourself. If he is a confident and outgoing guy, it is easy to slip into his routines – doing what he wants, seeing his friends. By all means do this but keep time for yourself. Go to your spin class, have your sofa night/ girls' night out. Remain a bit elusive at the start – the chase is the best bit!

- Only you know you, there aren't any hard and fast rules. Your heart is your own, so don't let others get involved and stick their noses in.

- If he doesn't give you butterflies, move on. You can't force chemistry and if it isn't there at the start, it never will be. Never allow yourself into the friend zone – that's a recipe for disaster!

- In the words of Janet Jackson, 'Let's Wait a While' – don't rush things and keep a cool head. DO NOT be that girl who doesn't call her friends for six months, remember that you hate that girl! You don't have to spend every minute together to be in love. Don't forget your friends as you will need them even if you do get your 'happy ever after'.

5

Break-ups and Heartache

We both knew deep down things weren't going well but, you know what it's like, you carry on because that's what you know and because it is easier than confronting the issues. That's where me and Joey are really different: he takes everything to heart so much. Even if we had a little row about something stupid and I'd got a bit stressed and raised my voice, he gets all hurt and ends up telling other people our business, which gets them all involved and means everyone feels they can stick their nose in and have a say whenever they want. We were stuck in this routine of working hard, playing hard and taking it out on each other and we were both under so much pressure. Joey felt trapped by the show and all the pressure on us being the 'perfect' *TOWIE* couple – we were the only couple who hadn't cheated and everyone wanted our 'happy ever after'. We weren't like Mario and Lucy, Ricky and Jess, Danielle and Locke, Ferne and Charlie – dogged by constant cheating rumours and disrespectful behaviour. Whatever our issues, we were always faithful. I know he meant it when he finally proposed, but I also know that he did it because there was so much speculation and pressure. You can see it if you watch it back, he's so stressed out! And soon there were so many rumours flying around it did my head in. I wonder sometimes if the fact we took things slower than other couples was a good or a bad thing. At the start I remember thinking to myself: 'Don't rush to move in together' – there really isn't any race. I remembered a conversation I'd had with a girlfriend a while before, where I'd wisely told her: if he's as right as you think then you will be together for ever. Spend a few nights apart and not the whole weekend together, keep some head space and keep things fresh and exciting. I like to think I was talking from experience with Joey, we never actually moved in together despite how long we were together and I think there was always something deep down stopping him. I put pressure on him to move in together but I felt, at times, when it came down to it, that he was scared of the crunch. Things would have been so much messier if we had split and had to sell a house and stuff – it was hard enough without all that added stress. The whole moving in was a step we didn't take and it was the opposite of moving too fast, it was more like we missed the moment completely. Maybe the warning signs were there and I just ignored them.

The show was also in a period of change around then. There were new producers and, to be honest, they seemed to have lost touch with all that defined *TOWIE* for its audience – they didn't really seem to have a clue what we were all about and it was someone's bright idea to introduce *TOWIE Live* in the middle of Series 7, which is when I almost became Joey's fiancée the first time around. Joey later told me that the new producers called him up and casually asked if he wanted to propose to me on the live show to give them their big finale. In fact, the implication was do or die really – propose or finish it with me so that, either way, they got their cliffhanger. I only found this out later when Joey broke down and told me this is what had happened. I had no clue whatsoever that this conversation had gone on, and being such a closed book he didn't tell me until much later. Looking back it is hard to see why we let them have so much sway over our real lives, I mean, who gets engaged because their work tells them to! But when you are in the groove of a show ruling everything, it is hard to have clarity. That was typical – there was always the promise of a big storyline and then the anxiety that kicked in if you turned it down – you worried that you had sabotaged yourself and the possibility of standing out. I think it is impossible to explain really without sounding a bit mad and fame-hungry – I am aware that we aren't long-standing members of my favourite soap operas like *Coronation Street* or *EastEnders*, but the truth is we all (most) worked hard and deserve to be applauded for that. Being on *TOWIE* wasn't a free ride; we had to put in what we got out. Towards the end you get savvy, but I didn't let the show control my life.

Joey and I had obviously talked about marriage and babies, it was what we both wanted eventually, or I thought it was, and when you are in any long-term relationship, you make plans and believe it will go the distance – no couple would make it past the first date if they didn't! No one wants to feel like they are wasting time for no reason. We were up and down and arguing lots but the endgame was always about being together. I said it a lot – I couldn't imagine doing the marriage and babies thing with anyone but Joey, and it has taken a while to get over that.

Anyway, it was a nightmare. It was all so awkward, Joey couldn't stop shaking and wouldn't look me in the eye. I really had no idea what was going on, just that everything with Joey seemed really strange. I don't think he did either as he wasn't the best at thinking things through. In the end the whole thing just fell flat as Joey lost the plot and walked out on the scene. I didn't blame him one bit, but it wasn't a nice situation for me. I felt really humiliated and it got me questioning everything again.

Despite the obvious pressures put on him by the show, it didn't stop his family, his cousin in particular, from blaming me for messing with his head and putting pressure on him when nothing could have been further from the truth. I knew we were far from properly settled enough to get married right at that minute and still had lots to work through – plus Joey had a lot on with the opening of his shop. I feel proud of the way I supported him through the opening of Fusey, to be honest. I am not sure he could have done it without me and I mean that in the nicest possible way – if you look back at the episode where the shop opened, it is fairly obvious that he doesn't really know what is going on! I know he would agree that we were a great team and I was so happy to give him all the tips and pointers we had picked up whilst opening Minnies – we had learned so much along the way – and it was a good feeling to be able to give that advice to Joey and really support him. We went to all the meetings together and I helped pick the stock and wanted to do whatever I could – in truth, I couldn't have been prouder of him.

I planned a romantic trip to New York to help celebrate us and also his big step in opening the shop. It was a belated birthday present and I knew it was somewhere he was super-excited to go, so I thought going at Christmastime, in the snow, would be extra romantic. A bit like Carrie and Big going around Central Park in a horse-drawn carriage, with a blanket over our knees and then sipping cocktails in cosy bars . . . Except it wasn't like that in the end, mainly down to a huge row all about Mark Wright and a scene set up by *TOWIE* producers to lift the storyline when Joey was out of the picture filming *Splash!*. Joey was filming the two shows at the same time, but very much knew there was nothing to worry about. It was a tiny scene that the producers sent Mark back in for. The whole thing was a storm in a teacup, but jealousy was capable of overwhelming both of us and the producers knew that and used it totally to their advantage. The infamous 'Mark' episode was airing in the UK when we were in New York and the night it went out, Joey spent most of the time checking Twitter like mad and going off on one that Mark was making a mug of him. He was calling all his mates back home and asking them to recite who said what and of course they were winding him up with comments like:

'It doesn't look great, mate' and 'He's all over her, she's loving it.' Then he called his manager, Dave, who seemed to make the whole situation ten times worse with what he said, though I didn't hear what that was. Joey was going over every detail and just went on and on – wanting chapter and verse about what I had said to Mark, what he had said to me – then he started reading out tweets to me from viewers. There was an explosive row which ended with me storming out of the hotel to get some air and calm down.

I went outside and sat on the edge of the big stone wall outside the Plaza just sobbing, I couldn't believe he was ruining my surprise over a perfectly innocent scene on the show, I had literally opened the door, said hi to Mark and closed it again. I went over and over it in my mind – for God's sake, who doesn't smile when they open the door to a long-standing friend when they are being filmed for TV! I knew I'd done nothing wrong, but Joey was a master at turning things round to make me feel bad, he had a real skill.

Anyway, he came out looking for me. I could see him straining his neck to look round and spot me, so I buried my head down further into my coat and pulled my scarf up. After a while, it was so cold I had no choice but to go back inside, so I went back to the room, climbed straight into bed and pretended to be asleep when he came in. He had more sense than to wake me up and try to carry on. The next morning, I got up and decided to pretend the previous evening hadn't happened, that was easy with Joey as he did exactly that after every row we had, especially when he was in the wrong. He took my lead and we both decided this was a fresh day. Not long after we left the hotel, Joey's phone rang. It was Dave. Joey went over the road to have his conversation in private. He stood outside the W Hotel and started to get agitated, pacing up and down like some caged animal. He was shouting so I could hear every word he was saying – I couldn't believe it – he was going over and over all the details from the conversation the previous night.

I don't know what Dave was saying to him but it was working, Joey was waving his arms about and going over the whole Mark Wright scene again. It was so weird, suddenly I just felt overcome with a mixture of deep-down sadness and real, boiling anger – why couldn't he see what I had done for him with this holiday, how much money I had spent and how hard I had worked pulling it all together? It was all designed to show him how much I loved him and how serious I was about us working, but he was destroying it, almost like he was deliberately trying to wind me up on purpose. If that was the aim, it was definitely working. There was something wrong with him that he had this need to destroy good things and make me out to be the bad one, it felt like sabotage. I could hear him asking the same questions over and over:

'Did she look happy to see him?'

'Was she smiling?'

'Did she touch him, did they kiss?'

'Did I look like a mug?'

Was he mad?! If I had genuinely been flirting with Mark I could understand it – touching him or giving him coy and flirty smiles, I get that would be disrespectful when I am going out with Joey and of course he would feel mugged off. But I OPENED THE FRONT DOOR ON CAMERA AND SAID HELLO AND GOODBYE, I wanted to scream at him. That was it, I couldn't stand that he was ruining this on purpose so I ran over the road towards him, possibly the fastest I have ever run! We were right in the middle of one of the busiest parts of New York and I was running straight at my boyfriend. All I wanted was for Joey to get off his phone and enjoy the amazing trip we were on. I just remember shouting at the top of my voice:

'What are you doing, you idiot, why are you ruining this?'

It wasn't my classiest moment but all I wanted was for him to stop, irrationality is the most infuriating thing in the world. The next thing I know a policeman approached us, tapped me on the shoulder and asked in a cute New York accent: 'Is everything okay, Ma'am?' It was so embarrassing and I was still shaking with anger. I told him that I was fine and tried to pull it together. Joey, having started the whole argument in the first place and gone out of his way to ruin the day, was now crying.

Again, I felt like I had two choices, I could carry on the row and ruin yet another day, or I could cuddle and make up and try and salvage what was left, so that's what I did. We kissed and made up and went to Ground Zero, which obviously put all our ridiculousness into perspective. I thought a lot about things as we stood there looking at this extraordinary sight.

The whole thing caused so much aggravation for us, for

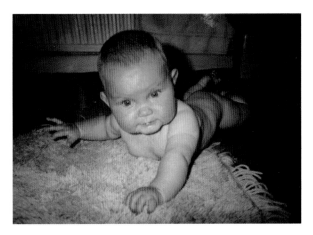

Me as a baby, aka 'Melon Head'!

I've always loved playing dress-up.

My lovely mum and me. She's always been there for me and is such a rock in my life.

Cute!

That's me on the left holding a cup of tea — I loved tea from a young age! My big sister Billie is only a few months older and we've always been really close.

I'm not sure Lucy will forgive me for this
one! This is when we were teenagers.

Billie and her partner Greg welcome my gorgeous niece Nelly to the family, and I learn to be Auntie Sam!

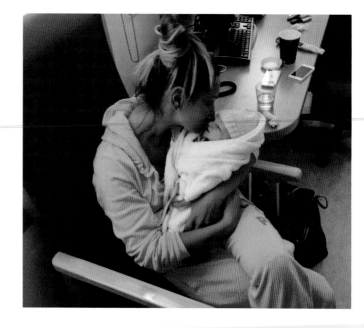

Baby Nelly is the most adorable thing ever and has brought so much joy into our lives.

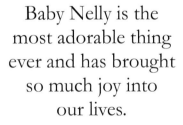

On holiday with the girls in Dubai.

In LA with Kim K.

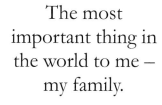

Five generations!

The most
important thing in
the world to me —
my family.

Back in our *TOWIE* days – my former
co-stars Billie, Lucy, Ferne and Arg.

me, it was so hard to know what to do – we were a couple with a life off screen, with friends and family, but we had to live by the rules of what we were prepared to share on screen. It also didn't help that Joey seemed addicted to the drama and angst the show could cause and even if it wasn't there, he went out of his way to create it.

After New York, it was a bit like walking on eggshells between us, we were on our best behaviour. I think we both realized that things were hanging in the balance. That Christmas was our first proper Christmas together and I wanted it to be really special. Christmas is such a big deal for our family and we like to do it in style with all our traditions. That year we gathered round at Billie's on Christmas Eve for amazing food and drinks, we were all cosy in our new PJs and sitting round the tree, surrounded by wrapped presents with Christmas music in the background. Joey had been invited but from the minute he came in I could see he wanted a scene and he certainly made one – and then promptly stomped off to sulk in his car, which was sitting on Billie and Greg's drive. I was mortified that the evening was being wrecked by him being so disrespectful. It was freezing so Greg put his coat on and went out to Joey to try and mediate and get him to come back inside. He was out there in his car without a coat, just running the engine on the drive. It was so bizarre. Greg ended up staying out there ages to try and coax him back in so we could salvage some of the evening. From that night on I don't think there has been any love lost between him and Greg, as far as Greg is concerned, that kind of behaviour is a million miles away from how any decent man should ever behave. It got me thinking about what I should put up with but, as ever, my family were amazing, they didn't say a word about it to me. I think they also knew that I'd snap eventually and see the situation for what it was sooner or later. My mum said afterwards that she always knew I'd see sense, but it must have been hard for her at the time.

Things didn't really get any better the next day. We both had Christmas dinner with our respective families and Joey was due to come to mine in the evening, and said that he would be there to eat with us. I had said it really didn't matter if he wanted to spend the time at home, I understood completely that it was family time, I wouldn't have left my family to go to his, but if he wanted to then he was more than welcome to come to Billie's. He was adamant that he wanted to spend it with me and my family and that he would be there for supper. So there was a place set at the table and we hung on for him to arrive, except he didn't. Everyone kept looking at me as if to say, 'When can we start?' and I just didn't know what was worse, to keep everyone waiting and him not show up, or to start eating and him to arrive late and get the hump that we didn't wait for him? In the end he solved the predicament by simply texting to say he wasn't coming at all, the message coming through well after he should have been there. He didn't even pretend to make up an excuse, he just said he was going to give it a miss. It was so rude, I was fuming that he was treating my family this way.

I hadn't put any pressure on Joey to come to us on

Christmas Day. He had said he wanted to, but one thing about him is he can't handle any pressure, and I think this got to him, being torn between pressure from his side and then feeling he had to come to mine.

Anyway, he did turn up later on and immediately picked a row, even though he'd been the one to behave terribly by being a no-show. And when he did eventually arrive, he wasn't exactly full of Christmas cheer; in fact, he walked in and sat down without so much as even acknowledging my family. He said a brief hello but that was it. My whole clan was there, including my Aunty Libby and all the kids, we'd had such a nice day and now he really wasn't doing much for the vibe. He told me he had a present for me but then he wouldn't actually give it to me, he kept patting it and then deliberately putting it away, like he wanted me to beg for it. He was wearing a huge designer watch and it turned out that my present was a matching one. He wasn't exactly one for showering his girl-friends with gifts. Anyway, we went upstairs for some privacy and, of course, we started rowing – the amount of tension he'd caused over the last forty-eight hours was unbelievable and it was bound to come out. He started on my family and the fact that he'd felt under pressure to 'perform' over Christmas and that his cousin felt I was putting him under pressure to be with me when he should have been with his own family. That was it, the mention of her name and the fact she had been stirring things just set me off. I hold my hands up, at this point I wasn't happy with how involved she was being so I did go to town a bit on her. We were on the landing screaming at each other, with my poor family downstairs on Christmas night trying to be all happy and cosy! We were hollering at each other and having a row right at the top of the stairs, when we lost our footing. I can't be a hundred per cent sure if he pushed me or not, to be honest, things were so heated it could have just been that we both lost our balance. By now his moods were so erratic that I had no idea what he thought was normal any more, and maybe coming round to mine in a bad mood on Christmas Day would have been normal in Joey's world. But one thing is for sure, his mania and madness had ensured I had the worst Christmas ever.

The New Year arrived and I decided it was time for a clean slate. I know it sounds weird, but despite everything, I really loved him and I thought we could make it. I look back now and I recognize the mind games he played, he was so good at it I didn't even notice. He had this amazing ability to make me feel like things would all be okay if only I tried a bit harder to understand him. In his mind it was never his fault, ever.

Things rumbled on but, little did I know, he was making plans to pop the question. After everything that had happened, it was the last thing that occurred to me, and he had enlisted Mum and Billie to help smooth the way. In fact, Billie had seen and approved the ring. I still don't really know what Mum thought deep down, even now she won't go into it in any depth, she will just vaguely say she knew it would be okay and that I was smart and strong enough to make the right decision. Billie has told me that Mum was worried but, at the same time, adamant she wouldn't be one of those mothers who muscled in. I think she knew that I wouldn't settle for a life like that, where I was really unhappy. She had drummed that into me because of what had happened to her with my biological dad.

Before I knew it we were on our way to Dubai again for the show, but without the rest of the cast. I genuinely had no idea what was coming, although Joey did seem a bit jumpy and distracted, but to be honest, he could be quite up and down anyway, so I didn't think too much of it really. I wasn't told what was going on, just to bring my passport and pack some clothes. I only found out our location when we arrived at the airport check-in desk, although I did have my suspicions. Before we got there, I did think it was out of the ordinary that he was whisking me away so romantically, but there had been a lot going on so I just put it down to him really trying hard to make sure I knew we had a future together.

One night, he organized a really romantic dinner on the rooftop of our apartment and, as we sat and sipped champagne, I felt so happy. Joey looked so handsome and he had planned a lovely evening but, all of a sudden, he started crying and I could see his leg jumping up and down under the table. He kept wiping his palms on his trousers and blinking a lot. To be honest, he was starting to worry me and I really hoped this wasn't a re-run of the disastrous *TOWIE Live* episode where he had just walked out. I remember asking him if they were happy tears and he nodded, then the next thing I remember he was down on one knee holding out the most beautiful engagement ring and asking me to be his wife.

I didn't hesitate. 'YES, of course I will!'

We were both shaking like mad and hugging and kissing – I genuinely forgot that the cameras were there and truly couldn't have been happier. No matter what we had been through, I loved Joey, I really did. I wanted to be his wife more than anything.

Once the bubble of Dubai and the proposal were over, we set about organizing our engagement party – well, actually there were two parties – one for real and one for the show. Joey was late to our private party as he was stranded in Dubai on a PA, but he made it in the end and everyone was on their best behaviour, trying to be civil and happy for us.

I understood there was very little he could have done about being late, bar flying the plane home himself! But it did cast a bit of a shadow over everything. I won't lie – I wasn't very happy. He said he wanted to do a speech. He got really nervous speaking in front of people so I was worried he would lose his nerve and break down with the emotion of it all – especially after the exhaustion of travelling, but he was okay and said some really sweet things about us and our families. I am not sure if he was trying to paper over the cracks of the fact that his family hadn't really forgiven me for the Dubai incident and weren't exactly thrilled that he had asked me to be his wife (although I will give credit where it is due to Frankie, she had been keeping well out of it and I think understood that what went on between us was between me and Joey, and that we were both adults who could wind each other up), but he kept mentioning his new cousin. I said to him, 'Stop walking

94

around with your new cousin, I am your wife-to-be.' His response was, 'That's my family.' He kept welcoming him to the family in his speech, even though this guy wasn't even really his family. That was the first night Joey had met this cousin. After that night I never heard of Joey seeing him again. The atmosphere started to turn a bit sour. I am not sure if it was jet lag or if, for whatever reason, my mates were annoying him, but he really didn't want them there. They had been my friends off camera for ages, my gay gaggle of mates who had stuck by me through thick and thin, but Joey wasn't really in a welcoming mood towards them, in fact, he made it clear that they weren't welcome.

In the end, as was often the way, it caused a big argument. I understood he wanted it to be me and him on our special night but I was also desperate to share it with our dear friends and thought he would be too, that's what normal couples do – celebrate their happiness with the people closest to them. Plus, I don't like rudeness of any kind – especially not towards my close mates. A row was a row – the difference was that this was supposed to be our engagement night!

I ended up going off with my mates to put some distance between us so we could both cool down, not exactly the most romantic of starts to life as future Mr and Mrs Essex, but I also knew it was the best way to diffuse the situation. I was feeling ground down by the fact that every big or important moment seemed to be ruined by Joey, like it was a deliberate attempt to control and upset me at every turn. I desperately wanted this night to be a happy one – I was feeling content and wanted to share that, whatever mood Joey was in. It was clear the party was coming to an end, but I thought if we stayed around a crowd, we would be extra civil and it would all blow over in that way it does when you have company and you have to keep up appearances. So I took a group back to Joey's flat, where I was staying, and we had a few drinks. Joey came back and insisted they all leave. He made it so awkward that there was no option but for my friends to leave, and there was no way I was going to make them leave and stay myself. I could see he was clearly determined that neither one of us would enjoy the night, so I told my mates we should leave and go back to mine. Joey was being so rude, I was mortified. He stomped off to his room and was, I thought, getting into bed. When Joey realized that I wasn't going to just cry and get into bed next to him because he was sulking, he ran out into the street after me, without any trousers on, screaming that he wanted me to stay. Looking back, I should have stayed and sorted things out, but it was so embarrassing, especially on what was supposed to be a night of celebration. But most of all it was exhausting – his mood swings that were more and more erratic, the tears and tantrums, the rudeness, the rows and silences. It felt like two steps forward and eight back. But when it was so public like that, on the street and in front of my mates, it was hard to put on a brave face. I went inside with him for a quiet life – what else could I do? It was our engagement evening. We finally went to bed, but in the morning I could barely contain my fury. When would it end? We couldn't even get through our engagement party without a ruck. The night had ended with Joey smashing my phone in anger.

We were scheduled to film the show *Mr and Mrs* the day after the party – which would have been bad enough with a hangover, never mind the awful cloud over us after such a showdown row. Neither one of us wanted to do it, though we are both very professional people and would never just have pulled out, despite us both threatening to do so to our respective managers. In the end, our need to fulfil our commitments won over the need to sulk with each other and we both got in the car and went to London to film the show. The irony was not lost on me – we were on the way to film a show that was all about how well you knew your partner and how compatible you were as a couple – you couldn't make it up! We travelled all the way there in silence. The only reason we were anywhere near each other was because we were contracted to be. We got there and were both all smiles with the backstage producers and runners – I guess that's reality TV training for you – no one would have known we couldn't stand the sight of each other! We were standing backstage and waiting for our names to be called, when as we stepped forward Joey hissed in my ear: 'Sam, I just want to say, you're fucking mental. Mental and awful. There must be something seriously wrong with you.'

Just what everyone needs to hear as they are about to film a TV show about being a couple!! The funny thing was that we won hands down. It seemed we knew everything about each other, except how to get on. I answered the questions based on how I knew he would answer them. Behind the scenes we had one of our biggest crisis moments ever, but on screen we were all smiles.

But that was nothing compared to our disastrous trip to Marbella to mark the start of Series 9, which had started so well. We had a great flight over and landed feeling really happy – we were in matching T-shirts and feeling very loved-up, but the producers had other things in mind for us and alarm bells should have been ringing from the word go when we realized they were separating us into girls' and boys' houses. It was so obviously a tactic to get more drama to fuel the storyline, but we just went along with it. Pretty much as soon as we started filming, the atmosphere turned very toxic and the producers got their wish. One moment that stands out the most was the first time I put on a new bikini I had bought – I loved it and felt great in it. Admittedly, it was quite a delicate two-piece, with a frill around the bikini bottoms, but it was modest and pretty (and it had cost a fortune!). Anyway, I put it on and threw on a kaftan over the top and off we went to the beach. When we got there, we did the usual thing of putting down our towels and waiting a few minutes before stripping off. As soon as I pulled my kaftan over my head and sat back down on my towel, I looked up to see Joey glaring at me:

'What the fuck do you think you're wearing?' he growled at me.

'What do you mean?' I replied, 'This is my new two-piece, don't you like it?' I asked nervously.

'Like it? No, I don't like it. You look slutty, it looks like underwear for Christ's sake,' he shouted and, without another word, he picked up his stuff and stormed off to another beach entirely, where he sulked and sunbathed on his own for over three hours, before coming back and acting like nothing was wrong.

The girls all decided to go out to mark our first night there – we went to the Buddha Beach club in a group and ended up bumping into Joey's cousin, Charlie, who was there with a big stag do party. It was me, Billie, Ferne and a load of lairy boys, but I felt comfortable as nothing was going to happen – I was in love with Joey and had never cheated (I never would, not in a million years), plus I clearly wouldn't be doing anything with his cousin standing right next to me! Anyway, we were having a few drinks before Joey and I had decided to meet up later for dinner as we had been filming in different places all day and wanted to catch up. Rather unhelpfully I had no phone that holiday, so had to rely on others passing messages on, which didn't help when I was out and about in noisy bars unable to communicate properly with Joey. I had a few too many (it was the first night out after a long and tiring day filming and I wanted to let my hair down), and I know I should have kept an eye on the time but we were all just chatting and drinking and, before I knew it, I was late for meeting Joey at his villa. I borrowed Ferne's phone to tell him I was on my way but that I'd be a little bit late. It was no use – he was livid that I'd been drinking with the girls, livid that I'd been in a bar with boys (even though they weren't anything to do with our group and we hardly spoke to them), and livid with me for having fun without him. He didn't want to meet for dinner now, even though I was hardly late at all and my punishment for having fun without him was that he went out all night and turned off his phone until the morning. He claims that the boys held a party at their villa and that, as he was sleeping, a random girl who had nothing to do with him, crept into his room and stole his trainers from under his bed. As you do. Apparently Joey didn't even notice these shoes were missing and went off to attend a photo shoot the next morning, none the wiser. The girl in question decided to be 'helpful' and return Joey's shoes, by tracking me down to where I was eating with Billie, Jess and Ricky and asking to give them to me personally. Ricky intercepted, but the girl still came in and dumped the shoes right on my plate. Imagine if a boy had gone to Joey and given him my shoes. I hate to think how he would have reacted. That was it – after all the aggro, the pain, me, Joey, his determination to blame me for everything, I just went mental. I scooped up the shoes and marched up to where Joey was doing his shoot – I am not sure I've ever been so bloody fuming. I went up there and he could see right away that this was a big deal – everyone left us to it. He hid behind a pillar as I fired questions at him about who this girl was and why she had his SHOES. We ended up chasing each other down the stairs. How could he put himself, and me, in this position literally twenty-four hours after we had broken up? Whether it was true or not, it was utterly disrespectful.

Instead of sitting down as a couple and recognizing that

this wasn't a good way for us to let ourselves be, we allowed it to linger and it led to more and more rows. It also led to Joey doing his usual thing of talking to everyone but me about how he felt, especially Diags and his cousin, who everyone knew weren't fans of our relationship. I could feel it all coming to a head but I didn't really know what to do – it was impossible to get any real time on my own with Joey. He was acting so strangely too – aggressively and overly emotional about the tiniest of things. Not having a phone was hard but it was like he preferred not to make an effort so that it was bad between us and that would help make him into a more sympathetic figure. Anyway, a couple of days after Joey's night out, he turned up at my villa with the crew in tow. He proceeded to break down crying as he sat down and told me that he couldn't cope any more, that I was treating him so badly, behaving like a single girl, that I didn't respect him. It was full-on dramatic and they were filming every minute of it. He said: 'I love you so much. I just want you to be happy and I don't make you happy.'

I knew this was the end for us. Not only did it break my heart but it was the ultimate humiliation to be dumped by your fiancé on screen and then have to endure the rest of the holiday with everyone knowing – it was awful. I am a proud person so I decided to try to hold my head up high and put a brave face on it all. We were put on separate planes home. I went on a much later one with Arg, especially as I knew Joey had left his car at mine and I didn't want to have to deal with that when everything was so raw. He got back way before I did and obviously went straight to mine in order to get his car before we had to face each other. When I eventually got home later that night, I opened my front door to see an envelope on the side, addressed to me in Joey's handwriting. I threw down my bags, knackered and emotional from the flight and all the drama that had passed. I opened the letter and there it all was written down – how much he loved me, how sad he was about the way he had behaved and the fact we couldn't make it work, how much he loved my family, how much he wanted us to have the 'happy ever after'. It was a long letter and from the heart. I tried to call him, there was no answer. The next day I went down to his flat to see if I could speak to him face to face. Despite suspecting he was in, I couldn't get an answer so I had to leave. Joey is, at heart, a good guy, but what he is, is a master of manipulation – he knew just how to play me. I wouldn't know how much until he went into the jungle and turned his back on all he had promised.

When I had calmed down I realized that Joey hadn't cheated, which was a relief, but it wasn't just that. This is the thing that the boys from the show don't realize about all these girls who take to Twitter (or steal trainers) accusing them of cheating on their girlfriends. Obviously it matters whether or not they are innocent, but the point is that boys who are in relationships should not put themselves in those positions in the first place – it is totally awful to be that girlfriend reading about what her boyfriend MIGHT have done. These girls want fame and money and they want it however they can get it. It doesn't matter if the rumours aren't true – they will spread them anyway and enjoy getting paid for the privilege. That's the thing about rumours, they spread so much faster than the truth. The awful thing is that the truth becomes kind of relative when you are faced with public humiliation and, for me, being dumped on TV was very much up there as one of the most humiliating things that has ever happened to me. My heart was broken and he knew exactly what he had done to me. Throughout all my relationships with Joey I was made out to be the bad person by the media and the people around him. All I wanted was to care for him and love him but I couldn't ever get that into his head.

Break-up recovery tactics

- Put away any cards or letters he wrote you, along with anything he bought you.

- Don't re-read text messages or emails he sent and DO NOT stalk him on social media either directly or through mutual friends! This is so tempting to do, but until you are stronger, it will not help. Seeing him tagged at cool bars with new friends, getting on with things, will only make you sad and angry.

- This is the time to have a 'friend' clear-out. If you do keep some mutual friends, do not allow yourself to ask how he is and don't get drawn into hearing how sad he is without you – it is his loss!

- Delete his number and, if need be, change yours. NO DRUNKEN DIALLING! I am guilty of doing this, who isn't!

- Concentrate on the good stuff – book a trip somewhere exciting, do the thing you've been too scared to try. Take it a day at a time and remember that the darkness will pass. One day you will be able to look at loved-up couples and not cry, one day it will be you again.

- Only you can make you happy, if you look to a man to validate you, you will never achieve your full potential. We are at our sexiest when we know what we want and we go for it, don't let heartbreak hold you back. Confidence, confidence, confidence!

- Remember the reality, not the edited version of your relationship – that will help remind you why you broke up in the first place.

- If all else fails, remember this: it wasn't meant to be. No great relationship breaks up, only bad ones do.

6

What Happened Next

However painful, life went on – I threw myself into the shop, my family and filming – and all my family and friends rallied round and I picked myself up. Before I knew it, it was October 2013 and we were planning our cast Vegas trip and I couldn't wait. The Minnies and my personal workload were through the roof, we were busy planning our new collection and shooting for the online new season. Me, Mum, Billie, Aunty Libby and the whole team were hectic and looking towards expansion. Our team was increasing, we had added new offices, and me and Billie were both being pictured wearing clothes all the time and they were instantly selling out.

Every time we were papped wearing a new piece – either at an official event or just out and about in Brentwood – the phonelines at Minnies would be jammed with enquiries so we would order in more, keeping the bulk of the stock for the website, and then ration it out. It seemed obvious to us that we needed to limit the availability of even the most sought-after garments so that we could try to retain some kind of exclusivity and I think we have achieved that. The really popular stuff, physical or online, had to be balanced with new trends and creating that 'must-have' vibe. To be honest we were looking to try to emulate the 'K Middy' effect – I mean, who wouldn't want that! The minute she so much as thinks about wearing something it sells out, becomes a classic, hits the *Daily Mail* sidebar and then gets put on eBay for five times the retail price as people become desperate to own it. Whether it is a Topshop dress, a Very skirt or a basic sparkly Zara necklace, once she has endorsed it, everyone wants it, no matter what the price or how hard it is to get hold of. Obviously I know we aren't princesses! But it is flattering to think people look at what we want to wear and how we put outfits together, and they want to look the same. Of all the opportunities that have come our way because of the show, this is the one area where I feel most blessed. Fashion has always been a huge love of mine and Billie's – what girl wouldn't want to sit down with experts and source stock, design online shops and then dress up and get photographed? It is a dream come true.

So this time of growth for the business came at exactly the right time – Billie was so loved-up and happy with Greg but I was back to square one romantically. Me and Joey loved each other but we just couldn't seem to make it work between us. I felt very flat and sad about the whole thing. Filming was about to start again and it would mean seeing Joey, being around him, dealing with the producers wanting to manu-facture situations between us. I had to really psych myself up for it. We were about to start on *The Only Way is Vegas*, so who knew what would happen? All I knew was that I was in quite an emotional place with it all and my head was far from sorted.

The *TOWIE* producers always have a way of making paths cross when it will cause angst, so I knew the next series wouldn't be calm. It was October 2013 and we were all packing to head out to Sin City. I was single and looking forward to quality time with the girls – it was a golden time in a way: me, Lucy, Billie and Ferne all out there together, drinking, dancing. But it is often the drinking that leads to the drama, as we know, and it all came to a head with me and Ricky after a fun night out for Jess's birthday. We went to see the Chippendales and had the best time. Obviously we got carried away because we were having fun but also because we were filming and had to make it interesting. Jess got called up to the stage and it all got a bit wild, but she would never have disrespected Ricky, especially not in public. Nevertheless, he went mental. Of course I was going to stick up for my mate – I was there and could see she had done nothing wrong. His jealousy was his problem and he had no right to ruin our night. He said some properly outrageous things that weren't aired in the end in case they caused offence and it really upset me. It was probably a combination of too much drink, tiredness and feeling lonely. There was only one person I really wanted to speak to and that was Joey. So I messaged him via Tom Pearce, as I knew they were together. That way I thought he could ignore it if he wanted. He called me right away and there we were, back to our usual chatting for hours about everything. It wasn't long before we told each other how much we had missed each other and before we were sharing a bed again. We did everything in our power to avoid the producers – we knew from bitter experience that if we gave them even a whiff that things were back on, they'd be following us twenty-four hours a day and the arguments and pressure were bound to follow. It was obvious though: we got caught more than once holding hands, in lifts together when we shouldn't have been, glances – you know how it is. It didn't take long for one of the producers to say something – though I was grateful that they didn't push it. The truth is that though they were always very good at manipulating the situations with us all to their storylines' advantage, they couldn't actively force you to do things you didn't want to and they knew that me and Joey would not play ball unless we were ready. Nothing was official – we were still technically over.

That said, my head was still all over the place. We had zero sleep and partied like mad, so when the producers decided to perk up my failing love life with the introduction of Elliott Wright, I wasn't really thinking straight. He made his entrance on the show in Vegas, when he attended Jess's twenty-eighth birthday party as a well-hidden surprise. I think he had been trying to get on the show for a while and he went way back with everyone – obviously he was part of the family with Jess and Mark, but he knew all the lads from when we were younger and they all used to hang out and get up to no good. He was an obvious person for the producers to get on board, especially as he was such a ladies' man. It was one of those things and we had a cheeky kiss, which was all fine until Joey found out. I know it wasn't exactly a great way to be – I mean, me and Joey were on–off, but on the other hand, it was so nice to be courted and get some genuine and uncomplicated attention and Elliott is very good at that! Despite what Joey said when he found out, that I was only doing it for airtime, that couldn't have been further from the truth. But Joey started reading all sorts of dark and complicated things into it. He decided that there was some great plot for me to make him look like a mug on TV and that I was going to deliberately play them off against each other. He got so paranoid it was impossible to try to rekindle things; he spent all his time running through various scenarios of how things might or might not play out. It was exhausting and just plain weird to be honest. For Joey it became about one-upmanship, pure and simple. To be fair, we both knew how the producers worked, there was nothing they loved more than a juicy love drama and if Elliott's arrival helped create that drama, then I can see it was an obvious route to more ratings. But that didn't say much for what Joey thought of me after all that time we had been together – I would never deliberately make him look like a fool on live TV. I knew what it was like, don't forget (his anxiety was ironic given he's the one who dumped me in front of millions of people!). So in the end Joey set off on his own mission – to get me before I got him.

So there we were in Vegas, all cooped up in the same hotel, with the producers throwing me and Elliott together whilst trying not to be obvious, with Joey watching our every move and pretending he didn't care. It was exhausting and depressing. One night I decided just to go out for a drink with Elliott. It was harmless holiday fun, it really was, but I also wanted to know if there was any chemistry between us. I mean, if it was going to cause all this drama, I might as well be sure! So we went for a drink and a chat, and Joey just lost it and started ringing and texting me non-stop. I really didn't see the point of making a big deal of it, so, as he repeatedly quizzed me about where I was and who I was with, I said I was with Jess and Arg, talking and enjoying our time together in Vegas. Joey's response came a few days later, after my date with Elliott, when he flew a girl he had previously met into Las Vegas for the end of our trip to make me jealous and to sabotage the scene where he was due to 'find out'. His reaction was rather extreme and, I think, a real measure of his state of mind. It was crazy to watch him walk in with this girl, just as we were about to start filming, I didn't know what to say. He had paid for her flight and everything, just to make his petty point. I couldn't help but think how ridiculous this was. To fly her in was a costly exercise, this was taking it way too far. He wanted to call the shots and knew that the producers would want to film his reaction to my date with Elliott earlier in the week. Even though it was clear he already knew, they were still aware it would make great TV and the viewers didn't need to know the timing, as far as they were concerned, Joey was finding out about me and El at the same time as they did. I felt that the producers were pushing the situation and wanting a bad reaction from Joey, tears if possible. The state he was in, I did worry they would get what they wished for.

The ironic thing is he could have got any girl to do it, but flying someone in took it to a whole new level. I didn't really know what to say and then, as the scene unfolded, it all came out – Elliott told Joey that we had spent the night together and Joey told Elliott I'd done the same with him. They were telling the truth, I had stayed with both of them but I didn't sleep with either of them! The next thing I knew, as all these accusations were flying around, this girl came into shot and grabbed Joey's hand to drag him off into the sunset. I didn't know what to do or what was going on – all I knew was that Joey was so obsessed with how the show might make him look he was forgetting how to behave in real life. At this point I was really confused on the show. The love of my life was showing an interest in me but how did I know his intentions were correct?

When we got back I tried to smooth things over with Joey – after all, he had totally got the wrong end of the stick. He wasn't having any of it and was determined to make it far more sinister than it was. Filming carried on and the producers had an inkling of what was going on, so of course my scenes with Elliott were doubled. The opening of the first episode post-Vegas was a party for Elliott to welcome him back to Essex from Spain. We were put at the bar together, having a drink and a chat. In came Joey, smirking and shaking his head, he came straight over and shook

Elliott's hand, trying to look nonplussed, asked him a few polite questions and then went over and stood next to Arg and the boys. He kept a fixed and very fake smile on his face throughout the whole episode, to be honest everyone thought there was something seriously wrong with him at that point – the cracks really were starting to show. I later learned Joey knew full well he was going into the jungle. He didn't want me himself but didn't want me to be with anyone else.

Obviously the storyline with Elliott played out on the show, though I have to say that Joey properly stoked the fire with his bizarre reaction so the producers knew they were on to a good thing and the cameras kept rolling, but off screen I obviously didn't want any ill feeling with Joey. I still loved him and my head was a mess. This is where the show can be really bad for your health – when the path you want to pursue in your real life doesn't fit the direction it needs to go in the show. Joey was behaving more and more irrationally and wouldn't have anything to do with me, so I went on another date with Elliott. The producers obviously wanted to tie up the loose ends with me and Joey, so they told us that we would be having a scene together where we 'met up' by accident and then ended up talking everything through. We spoke on the phone the night before, which I am glad about. Joey called and wanted the details of what had happened between me and Elliott, so I told him we had kissed and was honest with him as I knew he deserved that. We had a good chat about it and it became clear that we were both moving towards giving it another go. He suggested that during our scene I be the one to tell him that I still loved him and that Elliott was a big mistake and I wanted to give things another go. You can tell where this is headed, I suspect, but I didn't see it at the time, so I said yes.

The next day, filming was happening and Joey came to my house as planned. To be honest I was so nervous – I realized how much I wanted it to work again between us. I had spoken to Billie loads about it and I was sure he was what I wanted. I just worried that something wasn't quite right with him. I was standing there in my workout clothes in my house and opened the scene by telling Joey how much I wanted to give it another go, as we had discussed.

But suddenly he shouted: 'What feelings for me? You must have feelings for him [Elliott] as you kissed him. Did you kiss him again?'

I was stumped – he was making out like I had cheated on him but I had been a hundred per cent single. He had told me he was going to get back with me and now he was changing his mind – he was dumping me on camera again! I pushed him and told him to admit that he still had feelings for me, that if all this bothered him so much he had to man up and be honest about how he felt.

He came out with a killer blow: 'I think we just have to accept it's over.'

He trampled all over his promise but he had me over a barrel; I couldn't say anything in front of the crew as they'd know we had broken the pre-filming rules. He was enjoying his moment, making a mug of me on camera again. The cameras stopped rolling and Joey left, before coming back a few minutes later. The producers must have thought all their Christmases had come at once as, not only had he just dumped me on screen, but he was coming back for an encore.

I was so hurt, I just remember shouting: 'What the hell was that?' He started ranting on about me mugging him off with Elliott, of all people. I could see that it was driving him crazy, so I thought this was the time to tell him the producers had just made me film a scene with Lewis Bloor. I had been filming in the gym with Billie and he had appeared from nowhere – I had had no idea that he was joining the show. Joey believed me as it was clear that the producers were doing more and more of this now to up the ante. There was no doubt I was potentially getting myself in a lot of hot water telling Joey this, particularly given his emotional state where he was like a loose cannon, but I didn't feel I had a choice. It was all such a mess and the outcome depended on Joey's state of mind. One thing was clear to me, that we had to be honest and open with each other and stick together against the drama being cooked up. Joey just didn't seem to agree. It was so hard to be pulled in two directions like that, but the show had to go on and though Joey wouldn't be straight with me I had to get on with doing my job.

So me and Elliott rumbled on. We were papped out and about in Essex, where the headline in the *Daily Mail* unhelpfully read: 'Talk about moving fast! Sam Faiers spotted house-hunting with Elliott Wright just ONE week after he joined *TOWIE*'. It was a ridiculous headline and totally misleading – talk about looking like a mug who doesn't know what on earth she wants. The truth was that I was helping Elliott look at different venues for his restaurant business – he wanted a second opinion on the kind of place that would be right and he thought a girl's touch might really help. I mean, even by reality TV standards, house-hunting one week after a snog is ridiculous!

Elliott knew how to get the headlines as soon as he started the show, and was happy to go on record with a teasing comment. Referring to Vegas, he stated: 'We had a right laugh, and there was the right kind of chemistry there.' I felt torn – El was very attractive obviously, but I just wasn't sure. Of course I still had Joey on my mind and I wasn't doing it to wind him up. The truth was, however I moved on, it would be seen as hurtful by Joey. It is like having an office romance and then it going sour, but still sharing the same desk and watching the person you loved start dating someone else from the office – it is right in your face so of course it is going to hurt. Deep down, I knew that this whole Elliott thing couldn't work whilst I still had feelings for Joey.

Elliott is a great guy. He had just come out of a four-year marriage and had small children who meant the world to him – he is a brilliant dad and the kids come first, which is just the way it should be and I respect him for that. It takes guts to walk away from a situation which just wasn't working, like he did. Even though it meant leaving his kids in Spain so that he didn't uproot them, he knew it was better that they weren't in a toxic environment full of rows and upset. As he said at the time: 'It's one of those things where you try and try and you have to ask what the best solution is.' We flirted and had a kiss to test the water, but my headspace just wasn't right. In an interview with *OK!* magazine, he said I gave him 'a big pie in the face', which made me laugh. There was no big drama; it was just the wrong time. Whatever happened (or didn't in this case), it got him on to the show with a bang and that was a good thing for him.

After giving Elliott the boot and Joey deciding to give me the cold shoulder, the gym scene was coming up where I would be introduced to a 'surprise'. This was the scene I had told Joey about. So I got all ready (always a bit random to wear full make-up during a gym workout, but when you are filming you don't really have a choice – as ridiculous as it looks, it feels worse to be there in full slap, believe me!) and there I am with Billie 'working out' and in walks Lewis, or as the *Daily Mirror* described him, my 'teenage lover, Lewis'. I will admit I was surprised when Lewis joined the show and it wasn't ideal to have things awkward with Joey and to have to worry about Lewis as well.

Me and Lewis dated back when we were younger. You know how it is when you are young: you think you'll be in love for ever and nothing will go wrong! In fact, we were loved-up and had a good thing and then I started working for Mark as a club promoter at the Embassy Club. As Lewis himself explained: 'Her and Mark had been involved before and he didn't like the fact that Sam was my girlfriend. Then I heard rumours about Sam and Mark. I decided to save face in return by cheating on Sam with Lauren, Mark's girlfriend at the time. I didn't even fancy her but I wanted to get back at Mark. Very few people in Essex would bother to tread on Mark Wright's toes but I was one of the guys who didn't feel threatened by him.' That was a pretty stupid interview to give as it just made him look petty and ridiculous, though to be honest it was nothing in comparison to his awful behaviour when it came to his time dating Lauren Pope. I can't even look at those scenes now without cringing at how disrespectful he is towards her.

Lewis thought he could just stride back into my life and pick up where we left off, despite the fact that he cheated on me so close to home. When it became clear that we weren't going to happen, he tried it on with Grace, which resulted in a whole on–off thing where she rejected him in favour of Mario then changed her mind and asked him out again (which he LOVED!). It didn't work out so he moved on to Lauren and then proceeded to cheat on her in Dubai and moved in on George Harrison during a trip away to Marbs. For me, it is a world away from the guy who, when quizzed about us, said, 'I will always have love for Sam. Maybe not as a wife, but as a girl who taught me a lot about love, and taught me a lot about loving yourself as well.'

I remember the scene where I went on a date bowling with Lewis, where he threw out the revelation that in three years of dating he had never met another girl like me and that he was gutted for the way it had ended. I mean, I didn't really want to go into all that, especially as it involved a scene with

Lauren Goodger, who has been less than complimentary about any of us since she left.

Anyway, a few episodes rumbled on with me in some kind of 'love triangle' with Elliott and Lewis, with Joey hovering in the background, pretending not to care and the producers not quite sure which way he would go because no one could second-guess his moods. If things had been more pleasant with his family I would have totally been on the phone to Frankie or Chloe to make sure he was being looked after and to see if they had any idea what was wrong with him. Normally I could read Joey like a book, but he was cutting himself off from all the people around him who could have helped him and talked to him, and hanging out with a weird and, frankly, not very nice crowd.

I was worried that it would all come to a head with the upcoming charity auction, where I was being 'sold' to the highest bidder for a date. As we sat there and the bidding crept up, I remember feeling so disappointed that Joey wasn't even there. I had spoken to Billie beforehand about the fact that I really did want to give things another go with Joey, but that it was proving hard to get that through to him. Obviously I'd hoped we would talk at the auction, ideally away from the cameras, but then he didn't even show up and I had no idea what was going on and if he was even expected for filming. The money started creeping up as Lewis and Elliott got competitive and then suddenly Joey arrived out of nowhere. I genuinely hadn't expected him to show at all and didn't realize that he had struck a deal with the producers that he could come in at the end and bid as long as they promised he could win the date outright – there was no way he wanted to risk losing out to either of those two, especially given his obsession with us all trying to mug him off on screen. So in he swept with a bid of £2,000. I was so chuffed I called him my knight in shining armour and he called me Wendy to his Peter Pan. This was us at our best – all cute and loved-up – and I could see that the producers couldn't get enough of it.

As part of the winning bid I got another date with Joey – I was obviously hoping it wouldn't involve a dump this time but it did! He decided that he wanted to 'recapture' the feeling of when we first got together, which was actually cuter than it sounds. But after our first dodgy date at the local tip, he more than made up for it by taking me back to mine and showing me the little love den he had created. It was so unbelievably romantic and I loved it. He pulled out all the super-romantic stops he could – the place was covered in fairy lights and tea lights he had made himself (so he said!). There were sandwiches cut into posh little shapes. All my favourite food was there. It was perfect. But I could feel how tense he was. I was ecstatic that he had made such a huge effort and this felt like the Joey of old – kind-hearted and straightforward Joey – but he was holding back on me and I was scared that he was going to spring another on-screen surprise. I didn't want to move too fast. We weren't back together yet. So I decided to try to block out the cameras. After all, this might be my only chance to tell him how I really felt and push him to do the same with me. I was sick of all the game-playing for the cameras – this was about us and the fact that we had another chance to make a go of it – if only he would let me in.

So I pushed him to see if he wanted to make us official. He said that he wanted to try to get back on track but that he wanted to take things slowly. He used the really weird phrase 'friends with some feelings'. I couldn't work out what was going on – I knew him well enough to know that he was keen. I could see we still had that connection, and he could too, but something was holding him back. I had obviously heard the rumours that he was leaving *TOWIE* and flying to the other side of the world for a stint in the *I'm A Celebrity . . . Get Me Out of Here!* jungle but when I asked him he denied anything and said he didn't know what his manager was doing.

Places I love

Marbella

Marbs has always been home from home as far as I am concerned. From a really young age, me and Billie spent loads of time in Spain and lived there full time for a few years when we were younger, at one point with my mum and dad. My Nanny Wendy and Grandad Mick still live there, so it has a special place in my heart. Once we joined the show, it became clear that the producers felt it was a great place to send the cast for an annual special in the hope the sun and sangria would cause ructions and bad behaviour – I think they got what they were after! Some of the worst break-ups and bust-ups were filmed out there – I even got dumped on television! It is also the scene of Arg's crime when he first cheated on Lydia and where Mark cheated on Lauren Goodger with Lucy Meck – you get the picture. It really does feel like Essex-on-Sea, there are places to chill and tan and clubs to really let your hair down and party. Marbs is all about posing and that is why the cast spends so much time getting in shape before the filming starts. We all used to go on these mad binge fitness drives about six weeks before we flew out – it became comically known as 'No Carbs Before Marbs'. Ellie Redman came up with it on the show as a motivational saying when she was doing a diet and fitness programme for Arg and it just stuck with the rest of us (not that Arg really listened!). Back then in the early days of the show we were all so much heavier, the girls ate badly and drank through the filming days. We were all young and lived on pizza, fizzy drinks and white wine. I think everyone is a lot more conscious of nutrition now and much more toned and fit. I know Jess Wright and Ferne have stepped it up a gear in a bid to lose weight with regular workouts and diet plans. I look back at some of those pictures now and I cringe at how wobbly I look!

Even though Essex has slightly taken it over, Marbella is still posh and smart at night – people make a real effort and it is an expensive place to go; even on a girly holiday, you couldn't really get away with less than £1,500 for a five day break. I love La Sala Beach and The Ocean Club but as I get a bit older I prefer to stay in villas when I'm out there so that I am a bit away from it all – that worked out so well last time we all went out there and we took Nelly. It was so nice and peaceful to close the gate and chill by our own pool. If I do stay in a hotel, it's usually the Guidlapin or the Andulusian Plaza, which are near the centre of Puerto Banus. We used to always go to Hotel PYR. Back in the day, the boys would stay there too and get up to some pretty awful things. Luckily I've moved on from having to hear about all that kind of stuff now – it gave me nightmares! We all used to think we were *it* in Marbella, walking around with our shades on! Especially Mark Wright – going around the clubs like he owned the joint, doing his club nights, etc. I think being with Michelle has calmed him down a bit now, I am not sure she would stand for it!

New York

I took Joey here in 2012 for a surprise – we had both always wanted to go and so I went ahead and booked it. We behaved like total tourists. We ate so many burgers and hotdogs it was unreal, although that was when I started to realize that he probably suffers from OCD or some other kind of compulsive disorder. Whilst we were there he spent thousands on clothes. This was despite the fact that he already had a whole room stacked with trainers and a massive walk-in wardrobe crammed with designer clothes – half of which still had the labels on. Everything has to be folded in a certain way and facing the same way, he is weird about tying up his shoelaces too – he has this back-to-front way of doing it.

I would absolutely love to go back with the girls – not a massive group but just a few of the gang and Billie and Mum, maybe when Nelly is a bit older so that Billie can have a break. We could hit the shops, drink champagne, hail cabs and pretend we were having a *Sex and the City* moment. There is so much to do and see over there, it really is a super glam place that I'd love to get to know more.

Los Angeles

I have had some of the best times there, it sounds daft but it really feels like a place where anything can happen, where your dreams can come true. So much is possible – everything from movies to billboard modelling campaigns to endorsements, you name it. One of my best pals, Benny Hancock the make-up artist-to-the-stars, works out there and so he knows all the cool spots. I went to the Beverly Hills Hotel, Chateau Marmont, Soho House, and to the Playboy mansion last time I was there, which was amazing, but not as amazing as meeting Kim Kardashian, that was immense! I went out there after finishing with Joey to have a break and some new scenery. It is such a buzzing and happy place, the weather is great and it has an exciting vibe – I couldn't think of anywhere better to get over him and move on.

Dubai

I love this place. Grosvenor House in the Marina area is where I love staying. I also like the Jumeirah Beach bit and The Palm. I have been to Dubai loads of times now and you just can't beat it. The service is amazing, everywhere is five stars and you are so well looked after it is ridiculous – you never want to do anything for yourself again! The staff are always lovely and polite and treat you so well it is impossible to leave. Every trip has been special, but the one we had with me, Billie, Mum, Greg, Nelly and Jess Wright (plus her mum and dad) last November was the best yet. We stayed at the lovely Waldorf Astoria but also hired an amazing luxury yacht for a few days and just partied, swam, ate and laughed so hard. It was not long after her split from Ricky, so it was just what Jess needed. It was also Nelly's first time so far away from home but there were so many of us that it meant Greg and Billie could enjoy some time off together knowing that Nelly was safe with one of her family. Billie and Greg do it all themselves with Nelly – there is no hired nanny, only her real nanny. Nelly is so sociable and such a good baby, she loves a crowd and always turns on the charm – I wonder where she gets that from! Never mind worrying about what bikinis we were going to wear and if we were getting a tan, it was all about what outfit Nelly was going to be wearing, if she had her sunhat and was properly in the shade – how times have changed!

7
Jungle Joey

Whilst I was busy trying to read signals from Joey, Billie and my mum were convinced that he was leaving the show. To be fair, the papers were full of speculation every day about him being one of the 'secret jungle contestants' and I couldn't get a straight answer out of him – his mood was off the wall. I think this was the beginning of his intense paranoia, and it was typical Joey that he had someone in his so-called camp (excuse the pun!) clearly leaking information about him.

He had always been a favourite to go in the jungle and the producers of *I'm a Celebrity . . . Get Me Out of Here!* would regularly talk to a handful of the *TOWIE* cast. I mean, in December 2014 it had been between Gemma Collins, Chloe Sims and Jess Wright, and they went with Gemma (though I bet they wished they hadn't!). It always comes down to the popular personalities, the outspoken ones or the ones who will cause the most agg! When Joey was picked, I had been aware that they had spoken to the wider cast about it, just to get a feel for who was most keen – me and Billie used to laugh at the thought of us both going in there! Once the first round of chats was done, more serious meetings took place with managers involved, etc. It was always going to be one of our lot or someone from *Made in Chelsea*. Others from *TOWIE* had been fairly open about their early chats, but Joey was keeping very quiet. I think this was why he started to go funny and think people were selling him out. He couldn't understand where the press were getting their information from – it didn't occur to him that they were either just making a lucky and educated guess, or that he had a snake in his own camp.

So here we were – me and Joey. We were seeing each other loads off camera and I felt we were making real progress. We were back on in the literal sense and slowly getting there. I was aware that he had been spooked in the past, we both had, so taking it slowly was fine by me. We had become better at holding things back from the producers so they were just for us. We agreed to keep things quiet and see how we got on in our own time – or at least that's what I thought we had agreed. So I heard all these jungle rumours and took them with a pinch of salt. I mean, given where we were with our relationship, it wasn't like he was going to just go off to the Australian jungle just like that . . . was it?

And then the final episode of the series came and it was Chloe's birthday party. Joey wasn't there all day, then he drove up in his car. He wouldn't talk to me on camera and was being really shifty around me and then he called me outside. We had this bizarre scene where he told me he was going off, without mentioning the jungle, and that it was going to make us both a lot happier when he went away. He went on to tell me that he would always love me and that he would miss seeing my face – and then the cameras stopped rolling and I had no idea what to make of any of it. It had only been the previous night that we were making plans and acting like a couple; now he was filming a scene telling me he was, in effect, leaving the show and me behind.

We shot the scene – if you watch it back you can see that I don't really know what to make of it all – and then he asked me to join him in his car so we could talk in private and away from the cameras and people watching our every move. We sat there and he told me he was off to the jungle in two days' time. Along with all the speculation about whether Joey would be going in there, I also had to contend with the papers guessing who else would be in there and who the new 'Katie and Peter' were going to be. It was getting better and better! I asked if he would be getting with anyone whilst he was in there – even if only we knew that we were together I needed to know where I stood and whether the papers were going to be spinning all sorts of crap. As my mum had said to me the night before when we had been speculating – he owed me that after all we had been through together. I needed to know the truth when I was sat at home watching him over there.

We sat in his car and he was being weird. His eyes were glazing over and he was jumpy and nervy. I remember trying to put him at ease by trying to make him laugh. I asked him if we were still going to get married one day – I was only joking but he took it seriously and said he didn't know as he couldn't see into the future, and then I leaned over to kiss him and he went funny, saying, 'No, no, we can't kiss on the lips, only the cheek.' Then we sat there in silence before he turned to me and asked me to hand him my phone. I asked him why but he didn't say, he just kept asking to see it, so I got it out of my bag and handed it to him. He looked at it and turned it over in his hand – I speculated he thought I was recording our conversation, which was really weird. I tried to talk to him to see what was going on in his head. He was so paranoid it made no sense really. Then he turned his body round in his seat and said: 'Please, whatever you do when I'm in the jungle, don't sell any stories on me, will you?'

I didn't know where any of this was coming from – all I can guess is that the fact that everyone in the press had found out he was going into the jungle, when only a handful of people in his camp knew, meant he was paranoid that he would get screwed over whilst he was out of the country. That, combined with thinking I was taping our conversation, told me that his head wasn't right.

He kept asking and asking, 'I can trust you, can't I?', and saying things like, 'I have to know I can trust you.'

I knew this was goodbye. He told me that he would have his phone taken away as soon as he landed and I knew that there would be no communication with the outside world. It felt so weird given where we had been just a few days ago – it baffled me how quickly he could turn off his feelings. It still does.

I couldn't help but wonder if that was why we were in this mess of mixed signals. The truth is that for six weeks he had been courting me like 'old Joey'. He had been making me promises off screen that we would be together for ever, that we would have babies, get married, the whole romantic love affair, that I was his girl – the only one for him – and now he was leaving the show, jetting off to the jungle and about to embark on a whole new adventure without me. I didn't know what to do, so I went home to my mum and watched it all kick off, but even I had no idea how much I would be pushed to the limit, and how sometimes saying nothing really isn't the best policy – if there isn't any real information to be printed, the papers simply make it up.

The false headlines started almost immediately and, more upsettingly, they were accompanied for the most part by old pictures of me posing topless. Joey had barely landed in Australia before the first nonsense had been printed. These pictures were from years before, in my days when I was working at the bank and doing glamour modelling. What was concerning was that people thought because Joey was off to the jungle that I had decided to take my top off for attention. The silly thing is you could see in the pictures my face and body were completely different!

The *Daily Star*: 'Celebrity Jungle Pregnancy Riddle' – right underneath a picture of me in my underwear.

The *Sun*: ''Ave Sam of That' with a picture of me in a mock boxing pose in a bikini – a shot that was years old.

The *Daily Star* ran a whole article on page three, with me topless, as the headline screamed out: 'Angry Sam's on the Jungle Phwoar Path: she's off to confront Joey and Amy'.

This was the one that annoyed me the most – it made out

that I was choosing to be flown into the jungle for some ridiculous showdown to tackle Joey's 'romance' with Amy. Apparently I was so livid that they were getting together, that I was demanding a fee of £100,000 to 'stir up the camp'. When I got there, I was going to try to end Joey's relationship with Amy. The 'well-placed source' went on to say that: 'Sam's appearance will be sensational, it will be the mother of all jungle entries. You'll want to see the look on Joey's pretty-boy face when she walks in. He won't look so innocent then. He knows he's being disrespectful to her by making a move for Amy.' An insider added: 'Joey will be torn over who he really wants. Amy won't be too happy when his ex turns up and Sam will be putting everything on the line in front of millions as Joey must decide whether he takes her back or rejects her. It will make great viewing.'

To be honest, this went on day in, day out and it is the closest I have ever come to a full-on breakdown. There is something so dark and depressing about having no control over what other people say about you – let alone having no control over what national papers write about you, so that everyone is talking about you the whole time but what they are saying is utter crap. So many things about this upset me:

1. Whatever had happened between me and Joey, and however badly he had handled it (and he handled it very badly!), this was his moment. He was doing what he needed to. We were split up as far as I was concerned and we would stay that way. He had

moved on and was somewhere far away, doing his own thing. I was sitting at home, doing nothing to court the constant attention I was getting.

2. I looked like a mug, a little girl, the way it was being made out that I wanted to go out there all guns blazing and 'fight for my man'. It couldn't have been further from the truth – which was that I felt utterly humiliated by Joey: the way the last series of *TOWIE* had ended, the way I found out about the jungle, the way he had led me on, and now I had to watch on national TV as Amy Willerton found any excuse to touch him, do trials with him and rub suntan cream into his back. Truth be told, I didn't watch any of the jungle, not even one full episode. I didn't need to. Everyone on social media kept me up to date on everything, and I was seeing the front pages of the newspapers everyday.

3. By making out I was banging down the door of the producers to get me over there so I could confront him, it looked like I was desperate to get him back and I wasn't. I was humiliated enough.

I genuinely can't remember a time when I was so depressed. I even handled being diagnosed with Crohn's better than the time Joey was in the jungle. I cried for days on end, rowed with everyone, and basically I stopped eating. All my relationships became strained – I remember so clearly my manager, Adam, coming round and finding me in my tracksuit on the sofa, staring at the wall, not talking to anyone as he told me the phone was ringing off the hook. He still maintains that, despite all the busy times in my career – like *CBB*, the fragrance, the Very range – I was amazed by the number of requests for interviews, enquiries he had about appearances, what I was doing next, requests for quotes, and the amount of fake stories we had to tackle as they appeared in the press day after day after day. I just withdrew from everything and everyone and, above all, I refused to watch Joey in the jungle. What I did was become obsessed with how things were going to pan out for us and, more importantly, I became obsessed with being the thinnest I could be for when he came out. But before all the body image/Joey angst kicked in, I had to watch as his family started doing interviews to help him 'win', even if that meant talking about very personal things and dissecting our relationship for the whole world to pick over. Everybody seemed to be doing chats to support him but passing comment on me and our former relationship at the same time.

It started innocently enough with Frankie giving an interview to the *Mirror*, with an 'at home' photo shoot: '*I'm a Celebrity*'s Joey Essex is a fighter who overcame the death of our mum says sister Frankie'. I could see what Frankie was trying to do and, don't get me wrong, I've never really had an issue with Frankie, of all his family she interfered the least really and always understood that there were two sides to every story. Even if she didn't like to see Joey all upset, she knew he was immature and could give as good as he got. She was mature enough not to get over-involved as she had her own issues to deal with. In her initial interview some of the sound bites were, I think, to do with the fact that Joey kept being voted by the public to do the Bushtucker Trials. Though it is easy to see this as a sign the public loves you, it can also be because they want to see the person suffer – it is hard to tell. So at first the article concentrated on the lighter stuff: 'I don't know if he will eat camel's bits . . . he doesn't like fatty foods.' But then it started to get deep and uncomfortable, about things that Joey would never talk about himself. I could see that she was trying to drum up lots of support, especially from the 'motherly' crowd and that she was trying to show his vulnerable side: 'Losing Mum was the toughest thing that's ever happened to him, nothing can top that ever. He knows that Mum will be watching over him when he's in the jungle.'

She was asked how he would cope in there without his family and friends, and also with lots of time to think about missing his mum: 'This will change his life but not like our mum's death changed his life. The last time he got upset was at his perfume launch and he said, "I wish Mum was here."' He barely even spoke to me about it and I remember so clearly how upset he was when we filmed a *TOWIE* scene down at the graveyard. After the press found out that Joey's mum had died when he was young, the producers persuaded him to head the press off and film a scene at the graveside with me where he talked about his mum and how she had died. It was so emotional and very hard to watch Joey looking so tortured by it all.

Frankie also tried to put paid to the press deciding that Joey and Amy were the new 'Jungle Romance' couple: 'We know Amy but she's boring. She is very beautiful but Joey won't go for her. She's too nice. He likes a more outgoing girl.'

That was a brave thing for her to do, given how much the public love a blossoming romance and how much it can help with votes. It was reassuring for me to hear, but just a few days later Joey's dad decided to weigh in, though with mixed results as he sort of became a victim of the underhand press. Don was encouraged to discuss the 'Joey-isms' that the nation was seeing on their screens – his inability to tell the time, the made-up words and phrases and general lack of knowledge. As the nation cringed over Joey's occasional lapses of common sense, his dad told the world that Joey was 'bloody useless'. Don told everyone he was mortified that Joey couldn't serve tea, sell fish or blow his own nose. He said: 'I've been gobsmacked. I mean, I didn't even know he couldn't tell the time and as for not knowing how to blow your nose, I'm embarrassed to be honest.'

I sat at home, shocked. I remembered the look in Joey's eyes in the car before he went: the fact he was so adamant that no one spoke to the press. I was sure this included his family. But worse, every time they gave a piece to the press it fuelled more inaccurate stories about me, him and our relationship. It was getting out of control and the stories about me more and more ludicrous. Apparently I was heartbroken about Joey and Amy, and slagging her off all around town. I was also gearing up for a massive fight when she came home and rounding up all my 'mates'. I cried and cried on Mum and Billie – it was all so unfair. I was damned if I did and damned if I didn't. I really didn't know what to do – it wasn't just that I had promised Joey I wouldn't talk to the papers – I actually had no wish to talk to them. I didn't need or want any PR off the back of Joey being on TV. That's not how I worked and not what my fans have ever wanted from me. I like to think they support me because they like what I stand for and how hard I work, not because of who I date or because they feel sorry for me when he flirts on screen with someone else. So I decided to sit it out and told Adam to keep fielding all the requests for interviews, pictures, quotes and comments.

A few days later we heard that Joey's cousin was planning to do a story on me and Joey for the *Sunday People*, so Adam was all over it, trying to get an early look at the copy and exercise as much damage limitation as possible. To be honest, I kind of hoped it would go away – once we had been through it and corrected so many of the facts that were wrong, there was hardly anything left to print! But they still managed it.

I was so shocked when the paper actually came out. She had really gone to town. The headline read: 'Cousin . . . reveals Jungle star's rows with his *TOWIE* Ex: Sam would slap Joey and push him about . . . he's just a little boy.'

As if that wasn't bad enough, she went on to describe our relationship in detail, obviously concentrating firmly on the negative and even outlining our Christmas Day row when we were both at the top of the stairs shouting so much at each other that we lost our footing and both slid down the stairs. She said that I 'pushed him about', that I was the one 'desperate to marry' so we could become 'the next Katie and Peter'. Of course she didn't mention his dark moods. She said: 'Sam says everyone slaps their boyfriends but they don't. Joey says she slapped him more than once. He would bottle things up then come to me, burst into tears and lay it all out.' She goes on to (inaccurately) quote what happened during our last Christmas as a couple, when he came round to give me my present, the new watch. Apparently I made him come round to mine even though he didn't want to, and then we had a massive row over the watch (even though he wouldn't give it to me) and then my whole family started having a go at him! All this when Joey has always been the first to admit that my mum was lovely to him and Billie was so happy for us when we decided to get married. She had even helped him to choose the ring.

Despite all that, Joey's cousin couldn't help herself. She said: I've been blamed for them splitting up – but when Sam lays a finger on Joey it becomes my problem. He's like a young boy and Sam isn't like a little girl.

I couldn't believe it. I had to read it three times to really take it all in – this was the ultimate betrayal: a false article about my relationship, more lies without my side of the story in a bid to secure votes for Joey to win on the sympathy vote. Her story was totally inaccurate. I felt it was a step too far and totally went over the line. She claimed she had been misquoted by the newspaper and her agent relayed this to Lime Pictures. The sad thing was she gave another interview which was nearly exactly the same a year later, I find it hard to believe that you could be misquoted twice! It also brought up a particularly painful time for me, when the 'slap' had happened in Dubai and I had received such a backlash for it, with people only getting a tiny bit of the story, completely out of context. It had taken me so long to repair the damage done by all that; Joey still hadn't come forward to give the right version, and now his cousin was adding fuel to the fire, when she didn't even know the true story. But what really hurt the most was that through all this, I had stayed silent, just like Joey had asked me to. But now his cousin, Frankie, his dad, Diags, they were all coming forward with stories here and gossipy snippets there. It seemed everyone was allowed to talk about my relationship and my life – except me. Adam had been inundated with offers for me to spill the beans and I had been desperate not to be seen as selling Joey down the river. I discussed it with those closest to me – the situation was that I was being made to look consistently awful: first Joey dumped me on TV, then led me on that we were back together while at the same time knowing he was going into the jungle, and now he was on national TV all over 'Miss Universe', making me look like a mug for saying I thought we had a future. Finally, not only were his family slagging me off in the press, but now his cousin was making me out to be a control freak and someone who had made him too mentally unstable to be on the show and win. I couldn't let it go on, not least for my sanity, but also because this was my life they were ruining on a daily basis in the national press.

I was re-introduced to George Valentino, the psychic and spiritualist. I was wary at first. I am naturally quite untrusting when it comes to things like that, but slowly, after a few sessions, he started to help me see things more clearly. He was constantly telling me: 'The only thing you can change about the past is how you feel. By making the right connection, you can understand where you have come from and how you can shape your journey to a better future.'

He offered spiritual guidance and psychic insight that, whether you believe in it or not, certainly made me feel a whole lot better and in control. He had been on a few episodes of *TOWIE* before as Gemma, me and Billie had used him in the past (Gemma especially when things didn't go right in her love life would always seek reassurance from George that it was going to get better at some point). But this was different for me. I began to rely on George more and more to help me through this awful time. He was brilliant and I think I can safely say he saved my sanity. He had an angle on everything and, in particular, was able to talk me through what was going through Joey's head. Even though I wasn't watching him on the show, I thought about Joey every minute of every day and was desperate, obviously, to know if he was thinking about me. George was able to brilliantly deconstruct every little thing that might help me feel better – he was able to tell me about Joey's body language on the show and what it meant in relation to us, he was able to tell where Joey's head was with everything, and he was adamant that things were not, and would not be, serious with Amy, that his heart was still with me not in the 'showmance' with Amy. He told me that Joey wouldn't win but that he would come fourth. He would cut press pictures out of magazines and stills from the show and talk me through his body language. All of what George said came true, he told me the position Joey would finish and on which days key things would happen.

I know it perhaps sounds silly to some, but it was my lifeline and I clung on for dear life. I needed some answers to 'why' Joey was doing this and to know that I would be okay. It was so hard and the first week he was away was the hardest, but slowly George helped me pull back from the brink. I'd had nights and nights of no sleep. The first week of Joey being away was particularly awful as everything was just so public. I still couldn't get my head around the fact that Joey's stint in the jungle meant that I got more press than him, which meant I thought about him twenty-four hours a day.

Desert Island must-haves

All of this thinking about Joey tucked away in the Australian Bush away from all his home comforts got me thinking about how I would cope in a similar situation away from home (not very well, is the answer, but I would take the following to help):

- **Family photos** – I have got so many framed photos around my home, I would need little mementoes of those I loved, even if I couldn't see them in person every day, it would help.

- **My iPod** – it would be loaded with dance tunes, so I had music when I exercised, and would definitely have a lot of Sam Smith on it – that would help me chill out. I love his stuff.

- **A skipping rope** – that would help keep me fit and focussed.

- **False lashes** – lashes help me feel ready to face the world!

- **My pillow** – a girl needs her beauty sleep, even on a desert island!

- If I had to get through Christmas shipwrecked, I would definitely want a **tree** – I would just have to be imaginative with the decorations!

8

Skinny Minnie

was at breaking point over the Joey jungle stuff and my family were desperately worried for me. I tried to control my hurt by controlling my weight and I fell into a spiral of exhausting obsession and ritual. I knew the calorie intake of absolutely everything that I consumed. You name it, I knew, down to the decimal point, how many calories it contained. I started keeping secret lists of everything I had eaten and drunk. Having been curled up on the sofa for ages, not wanting to see anyone and not watching any episodes of the jungle, but having had to read about myself every day in the papers, I decided to distract myself with exercise. I quickly became obsessed with that too. Every day I worked out and pushed myself to the max, whilst consuming as few calories as was humanly possible. I was desperate to be busy and not think about what was going on in my life.

But, on the plus side, the endorphins did help me cope with reading stories about myself that were just absolute crap, it is so much better than sitting on the sofa crying, drinking wine and eating ice cream. Trust me, the best thing you can do is to look and feel incredible. The exercise may have got out of hand but, in a way, I think it really helped to distract me from all the drama going on around me.

I hated myself and hated what others were doing to me so, rather than being kind to myself, I made life more difficult. I know I was a nightmare to be around; it was only afterwards that friends and family were honest about how hard it had been to deal with me. For the first time in all the years we had been client and manager, I fell out with Adam. I was thin, moody, sleep-deprived and lurching from one low to the next. I was most certainly extremely down. Even if I didn't know it, everyone around me did. What I couldn't see at the time was that the best thing I could do was to nourish and help myself heal by looking after my mind and my body. It was weird because the exercise kept me focussed and determined when I thought I'd never be happy again. Now I truly look forward to my workouts, I love sweating out all the anxiety and stress. For me now, there isn't a problem I need to run away from with the exercise, it just enhances how good I feel about things and how strong I feel after everything that has happened. But back then, I was in a situation where I took things too far. When Joey was in the jungle and millions of people were watching him hook up with Amy, I started counting calories for everything I wanted to eat, and, more often than not, I then didn't eat it. From research I have done and what I have heard this really is a slippery slope and is often a path to people developing an eating disorder. I worked out every day, intensively, and that stepped up when I knew I was definitely going into the *Celebrity Big*

Brother house. I became obsessed with how I would look on camera. My view of myself became distorted and I didn't like what I saw. I never made myself sick but I did starve my body of what it needed, like some kind of punishment. Just before I went into the house I lost a staggering 23lbs.

Publicly I was saying that it was due to the fact I was on the 'heartbreak diet' after Joey and that I had piled on pounds comfort eating in my relationship. I remember giving an interview where I had my reasoning at the ready – that being with Joey was tough because he could eat what he wanted and never put on weight, that it was completely different for me as any extra weight immediately shows on me. That is true, I have always had chubby cheeks and when I put on weight any excess goes straight to my face, thighs and tummy. My face goes all puffy. To be fair, I had been horrified that summer of 2013 when I saw paparazzi pictures of myself in Marbella – I had my belly hanging out and I was stuffing my face with a cheese sandwich. That was just the start – my diet was bad whether I was on holiday or at home.

Joey and I ate so many takeaways when we were together, I would put on all the weight and he wouldn't. My weakness has always been Chinese takeaways: chicken chow mein, crispy duck pancakes, me and Joey had always loved sharing a big blowout order and I knew that had to change. But deep down I didn't have a healthy attitude to why I wanted to lose the weight and I did it in a damaging and excessive way. The truth was that I was starving myself and exercising for hours a day. It became a never-ending cycle and it was destructive and I was being secretive with those I loved – but nothing was as important as dropping the pounds and keeping them off.

I became obsessed with my body and my weight. I went from 10st 2lbs to 8st 7lbs – losing three inches from my waist and shrinking down from a size 10 to a small size 8. My diet was so sparse – no carbs, no booze, no treats, it was so miserable. Seeing me shed the weight also made some of the other *TOWIE* girls competitive about it. Suddenly they were all in the gym and banning carbs as well as trying to copy my more pared-down style, it was flattering that everyone was watching me so closely! That said, it didn't really help give perspective – that didn't come until I got so ill that I couldn't keep a thing down. Suddenly, what the scales had to say didn't matter at all.

My body had become used to my erratic lifestyle – being in the show had introduced a randomness to my routine and body clock – we were surrounded by crappy food and often it was cheaper to shoot the night-time and party scenes in the morning, when places like Sugar Hut were shut to the public. It introduced a really unhealthy attitude to and relationship with my body and food.

I started doing all I could to maximize the weight loss. Actually, despite the fact I was only doing it to get super-skinny for Joey, to show him what he was missing when he came out of the jungle, the exercise did eventually start to help my mood a lot. It helped me get rid of my frustrations and channel my anxiety into something positive. The ironic thing is I was spending so much time losing weight, I had no idea what was around the corner and that my health would have me at my lowest weight ever and so ill, the slimmest I would ever and have ever been.

I know everyone around me was keen that I understand that starving myself and being a stick insect for Joey's return wasn't going to solve anything. The truth of the matter is I had got over Joey and fallen head over heels in love with the gym. The other thing that did help was my decision to tell my side of the story – if Joey's camp could spill the beans on things they didn't even know about, I was going to take back some control and tell the truth – why should everyone else get to talk about my life but me not be allowed? So I finally accepted an offer from the *Sun on Sunday* – one interview spread across two days – this was my chance to tell it as it was. But I had forgotten the golden rule, that your words can be twisted to fit the desired headline and angle. My own headline wasn't great: 'Sam Faiers: Six times a night Joey was a real jungle tiger in bed. Then he'd fall asleep with his head on my boobs'. I know that every tabloid needs a good headline so I wasn't surprised.

I was asked a whole host of questions that I answered as honestly as I could. Looking back, I probably wasn't in the best frame of mind in which to do my big interview, but it was very much now or never – I knew I needed it to get back on an even keel. Of course it was sensationalized, that's what papers do and what journalists are paid for, so quotes like: 'She isn't the girl for him, she is not Joey's type at all and needs to stop acting up' were going to be picked up on when I was asked if I thought Joey and Amy would get married like Peter and Jordan.

I was asked a straightforward question: 'Would you welcome her to Essex after the show?' I was misquoted as
saying: 'She wouldn't be welcome in Essex after the show.'
Who would I have been to say she wasn't welcome in Essex,
I didn't even know the girl. I was being paid for the interview
so I was aware of my obligations to answer all the questions I
was asked in a decisive way. Given he was supposed to be
very much 'in lust' with Amy, it was obvious that they would
ask lots of direct questions about Joey's libido. The point was
clearly to work out if he would be missing sex whilst he was
cooped up in the jungle. I knew he would but I certainly
knew that Joey wouldn't be the type to do it with cameras
around – and I very firmly said as much. I knew Joey. He was
shy about sex and all that. I mean, he was like a little kid the
first time he saw me naked – he went bright red and got all
nervy about where to look!

I felt happy that I had been fair to Joey. There wasn't one
negative thing in there, not one. In fact, looking back at it, it
was a eulogy – I couldn't have made him sound better and he
certainly came across as very good in the bedroom. They
quoted me as saying: 'He was excited like a tiger in the jungle
around me, we were having sex six times a day.' To be fair, it
could have been a lot worse for him, especially given what he
had put me through. But the main thing was that the only
motivation to do the interview was out of necessity to put the
record straight and have my say – I would never have had to
do that if his whole family hadn't assassinated me. But even
knowing I was morally in the right didn't prepare me for the

backlash I faced, even from my own fans. I got over a hundred tweets a minute criticizing me for doing the interview on Joey. Everyone decided that I had sold out on him whilst he was in the jungle in spite of him privately asking me not to talk to the press, but no one seemed to remember that the only reason I had to do the interview in the first place was because everyone was talking about me, my former relationship and our private times. I was worried about the backlash so we accepted an offer for me to go and give my side on *This Morning*. This was the turning point and Eamonn and Ruth were great when they conducted the interview

But it didn't stop there. Obviously Joey's family came out en masse to stick the boot in too. Chatting to *Heat*, a 'friend' of Joey's said: 'After she said all of that in a newspaper, we all knew Joey would never take her back. He hates anything like that – it was such a bad move to do that behind his back. He may still care about her, but any feelings he had will be gone once he reads that article.'

Then Joey's cousin decided she wanted to wade in again, getting a 'source' to say she 'already had problems with Sam – it looked like they'd managed to patch things up, but now she thinks Sam's interviews have been really distasteful. Joey sees her as a mother figure and listens to what she says – there's no way he and Sam can get back together now.'

And then, to top it all off, there was Joey's dad. Don told *Now* magazine that Joey would be furious when he heard that I had sold a story about our relationship, that we should never have got engaged in the first place and that he would love to see Amy and Joey get married: 'I can definitely see him being happy with her. He seems at ease with her. I'd love there to be wedding bells. I get on well with Amy's dad.' How lovely for me to read, but also very sad, as I always had a great relationship with Don. Arg rang me to tell me Don was pissed off with me so I texted him and explained my side. Don was lovely and came back with support and apologized for what he had said. I know he loved me and Joey being together and was so excited when we got engaged, especially when Joey called him to ask advice on how to propose. Anyway, this all ended up being bullshit in the end as of course me and Joey got back together.

The irony was that when Joey came out of the jungle he resented me, but I truly felt justified in what I had done. I had done one story and that was my story and I had every right to defend myself against his camp and their war. My camp was a small one and I would never ever have asked my family to do anything on my behalf, though I knew that Billie and my mum would have if I'd asked them to. It was about staying true to myself. The fact is that Tom, Diags, Frankie, Joey's dad – even Joey's nan – sold stories, yet it all got turned round on to me that I was the devil for doing a 'kiss and tell'. My Mum, Billie and Ferne all turned down offers to speak and comment on our relationship and Joey's time in the jungle. They all managed to go without commenting and being paid to talk. But, in a weird way, getting angry about it gave me back some spark and I just wasn't having it. I think that's also when I realized that punishing my body wasn't the answer. Joey later told me that he thought about me all throughout his time in the jungle and when he left the first person he wanted to ring was me.

Any girl knows that we all have our low self-esteem moments – most of us are lucky that they come and go without us really noticing, but for some it is more severe. My first understanding was when I was seven years old and I started suffering from trichotillomania, more widely known as chronic hair-pulling, especially my eyelashes (this problem has stayed with me and very much inspired my range of false lashes). I have spoken about it before and touched on it briefly in my previous book. But I suffered a proper relapse during this time; my poor body was in meltdown. It is a confidence thing with me, as with lots of girls I am sure, the eating and exercising, and the compulsive hair-pulling. As I have said before, people with this condition do think they are weird and ugly for doing it and I am all for raising awareness by talking about it and helping others as much as I can.

Anyway, it all reached crisis point – I couldn't have felt worse in myself and I was still getting a fair bit of public stick – and then Joey and Amy were voted out. Joey came exactly where George had predicted he would (I obviously hadn't asked him about Amy!), but no one could have foreseen that Amy and Joey would leave the jungle at the same time, thus enabling them to have a good week of press in Australia that would add insult to injury as far as I was concerned. I knew deep down that Joey thought he was going to win as everyone around him seemed to have put that idea in his head. Having watched the clip, back you can see in his face he is shocked. And so it began: the Twitter campaign from him, the press interviews, the pap shots, the 'his and hers stolen moments' – it just didn't stop, but weirdly I started to care less. It was bizarre, like now that he wasn't hidden away any more and I could get hold of him if I wanted to, it felt less raw. Maybe I had done my grieving and had my fill of drama and humiliation. To this day I couldn't really tell you exactly what it was that made things shift in my head, but they did and suddenly I felt psychologically lighter. I think it helped that their message was completely confused from the very start – he was telling the press they were taking it slow and she was saying that he was 'like a brother' to her. I started eating normally again, exercising to feel good rather than to shed weight but, more importantly, I started to laugh again. It was a strange relief to hurt less. I felt like the Sam-and-Joey ship had sailed and that was okay.

In doing this book, I did obviously look at his book *Being Reem* and what struck me was how little you really know anyone. I mean, he was always sweet Joey to me and I know he loved me to pieces, but, in my opinion, he wasn't very gentlemanly about Amy in his book. I am sure her family don't want to read about what she is like in bed – that wasn't very gallant. George predicted all this would come as soon as they were out – that it would look to the world like they had found love in there and that Joey might even believe it himself at the start, but that his heart wouldn't be in it and it would fade away very quickly. George also predicted there would be a quick and deep shift in how I processed it all, and there was. It was a testament to how I had moved on that I was able to be pragmatic about how the press continued to stir things, even with headlines like the *Daily Star*'s 'Joey Essex in tears over Sam', where they claimed that 'heartbroken Joey Essex broke down and sobbed when he left the jungle because he could not get his ex-fiancée Sam Faiers on the phone. The first thing he did as he was driven away was try to call fellow *TOWIE* star Sam.' Well, that was news to me and just as well I didn't believe it as stories like that are enough to drive you mad. I stand by the point that comments made by people about Joey were unfair. It was branded that I have done a 'kiss and tell' on Joey, but how can you do a kiss and tell on your own relationship! Joey told me he had gone to phone me but had been talked out of it by people around him.

Suddenly it was December and it was manic – I worked incredibly hard with little time off, and obviously it is the month of fun with so many parties too. I forced myself to socialize a bit to make up for how miserable I had been. I knew I just had to get on with it and work has always been a great release for me. I really believe that distraction is the best policy. There was so much to be grateful for and so many opportunities to take advantage of now that I was feeling more like myself. I am normally such an upbeat person and it had been a scary experience to feel so low and out of control. This was the new me and I needed to re-educate my mind. I was desperate to keep busy and positive. It was weird, the last month had been so, so bad that there had been some days I couldn't imagine ever feeling normal again (though my mum was amazing and never stopped telling me I would be more than okay and that I would pick myself up because I was a fighter) and all of that just disappeared, exactly like George said it would. My new motto reflected a jumper I was photographed in: 'No boyfriend, no problems!' My life was my own and it didn't revolve around a man any more or the need to constantly try to make him happy, second-guess his moods or cope with the disapproval of his family.

During that week of post-jungle press, knowing when and what was going to happen, thanks to George, definitely helped me to switch off and something sort of magical happened and I was able to just find some space in my head for other stuff. George was adamant that good things were coming, more specifically that I would get a firm and exciting reality TV offer that wasn't connected to *TOWIE* and that, no matter what, I must take it. This opportunity would mark the beginning of new and exciting times and change my life.

But though I knew I had to push myself to move on, I also knew that I had been through a hard time mentally and physically, though I had no idea what was to come. So I said yes to *Celebrity Big Brother*, worked hard to get myself into a good place before I went in, and felt fantastic. Just for a minute I allowed myself a pat on the back for having got through the worst year ever and for embracing something scary, new and ultimately massively exciting. It felt like a smart thing to do on the back of having no control over what people were saying about me when Joey was in Australia. I'd had the world and his wife expressing an opinion on what I was like, what I thought, how I treated people, what a bully I supposedly was – here was a chance to simply show people the real Sam and talk for myself. It was a risk being in a show notorious for game-playing and psychological stress all in the name of good ratings, but in a way I was more qualified than most to put up with it I guess. I knew that so much depended on who else was in there with me but there wasn't anything I could do about that. I just had to go in there and be myself.

The first thing I did after saying yes to *CBB* was treat myself to an amazing new car. Then there was Christmas. It was a lovely day at Billie's (she is such a good cook and a great organizer, so everything was perfect), and then it was my birthday and I threw a Disney-themed birthday bash with a marquee and a DJ. It was amazing and a great way to say goodbye to a pretty crappy year. There were so many people there, including George Valentino, and what George had to say was, as ever, insightful. He told me that Joey and I would get back together, that there was lots of unfinished business. He also told me that I had a lot of 'snakes in the camp'. He told me that I couldn't trust them all and that there were lots who were simply out for themselves. George is a very talented psychic and helped me when I had lots of stress going on. Although we aren't as in touch now he will always be a great friend.

He also warned me to keep my cards close to my chest when it came to sharing information and details of what I was up to next. He urged me to keep certain people at arm's length and make a conscious effort to step away from all the negativity, that there would be good fortune but that certain 'friends' wouldn't be as happy for me as they should be. He was adamant that there was a lot of jealousy floating around and I should be on the lookout for back-stabbing and sabotage. I knew what he meant. I had been feeling a bit suffocated by it all – Essex is such a small and incestuous place full of drama and even when there isn't any people just make it up, and that was forming part of my need to break away.

I thought long and hard about this and actually had been thinking generally about making changes in the new year. I had been thinking it might be time to move on from the show. I have said before and will never tire of saying it, I will never regret the show – I had some of the best times on that show and it opened some of the most amazing doors for me. I never took it for granted and would never have made the mistake of thinking I was bigger than it. They had left the door open for Joey's return when he left for the jungle, but we all knew he wasn't coming back and there were obvious implications for me. The truth is that a lot of my profile in the show previously had been determined by who I was dating and I felt I had outgrown all that to be honest – there was no way I wanted to go back down the route of storylines like the Elliott/Lewis one. Things were shifting for me – I felt I was getting some good press attention now for how I looked, for hair/make-up/clothes and this was having a great effect on Minnies. We were doing so well. There were press articles saying how nice I looked and how well put together my outfits were and it was so nice to read those instead of the ones that talked about whether me and Joey were on or off. In the back of my mind, I wondered if it was time to leave the show behind and branch out a bit. I took the decision that 2014 was a year where I would invest in my own brand. I met with stylists and publicists to help take things to the next level. Laurie Hadleigh became my amazing stylist and I work closely with her each day. She has a fantastic eye for clothes and style and has taught me how to put outfits together. Thanks, Laurie. I also met the amazing Lauren Lunn Farrow, who looks after Katie Price's PR. Lauren was really on the same level as me and Adam and has become an invaluable member of our team ever since. I have to say though when I see her number calling my mobile I panic thinking, 'Oh my God, what have I done now!'

Whatever happened in the future, I was adamant that I didn't want to leave *TOWIE* and then do *Celebrity Big Brother* – after all those series, I didn't just want to walk off into the sunset one week and turn up on a different channel the next. I felt like I owed the show more than that.

But I knew I had a lot of thinking to do about my future on the show. Dynamics were changing fast: Lydia had left, lots of others who weren't originals or permanent cast members had been and gone, Kirk had come back and gone, Lucy had gone and so had Joey. It may not look it but filming is time-consuming and demanding, and it felt like all the other things that had come along because of the show, especially Minnies, needed more time and attention. I also didn't want to be the last original man standing, as it were. And I didn't want to get sucked into the bickering. It became difficult to get a word in sometimes when we were filming. It felt very much that all the relaxed and fun feeling was being drained. It felt far less spontaneous than ever before and that was hard if you had been in it from the start and you felt like the spirit of the show had been lost.

I still hadn't heard from Joey, and for that I was glad. All our 'conversations' had involved him slagging me off in interviews for doing a 'kiss and tell'. I was dying to hear what he had to say about his whole family making money out of him whilst he was in the jungle, but of course that was never discussed. Apparently he thought long and hard about calling me and had gone to call me a million times but, in the end, had decided not to as 'I knew if I called her my name would be used as part of her publicity machine' and I would just sell what he said to the highest bidder. If that was how he felt then I was glad that he wasn't trying to get into my head and spoil my *Celebrity Big Brother* experience. This was my time to do something independent from *TOWIE* and, after an awful end to 2013, I was determined that the new year was going to be a good one for me.

The day I walked into the *Celebrity Big Brother* house, I knew I was embarking on a once-in-a-lifetime adventure, though even I had no idea how dramatic it would be. Perhaps the fact we entered the house in handcuffs should have been a hint that it wouldn't be straightforward, though I never would have thought I would leave with a life-threatening and life-changing disease.

Strike a pose

Before I went into the house, I had a panic and realized it was going to be like one big red carpet moment with everyone looking at me. I realized I had to be prepared to be looked at from every angle possible. There have been many more of these moments than I ever imagined since joining the show and I know it is definitely important to work it to your advantage. There are a few ways to make sure you get it right on the night.

- Posture, posture, posture. Always hold your head up high, your neck should be down and back (boobs out a bit but not in a vulgar way). Look at how Victoria Beckham does it, she is such a pro with one hip back and the opposite leg out as far as it goes as well as pointing your toes. She achieves the perfect outline every time and always manages to look super slim and graceful.

- Cross your legs one behind the other, this helps to make your waist look smaller.

- Try and keep your face relaxed and don't over smile, try and be natural.

- Don't trip over! Try and move slowly and pick up any long hemline to avoid any accidents being captured on camera.

- Get your fake tan and make-up right. The orange stuff can be a nightmare. It is such a cliché that Essex girls can't apply it properly, after all, we invented it as a must-have! That said, I have had many a tanning disaster, so listen up and I could just save you from a catastrophe!

- Preparation is key: an even surface on which to apply the tan is a must-have so make sure you go to town with the exfoliation brush. Really concentrate on the dry areas like elbows, knees or ankles.

- Apply your tan the night before you go out – that way you can deal with any disasters and it has time to settle in without streaks.

- Moisturize all over and leave it to sink in properly – failure to do so will result in smears and this will not be a pretty sight!

- Use a mitt to apply, if you don't then your hand will be stained neon orange for all to see. Start at the top and work down, finishing with your legs and feet.

- Once you have applied your tan make sure you leave it to dry properly by wearing dark, loose clothing for a while afterwards.

- The best thing you can do to keep your tan once it is applied is to keep yourself moisturized. Apply body shimmer for the ultimate shine.

9

Reality Bites

Celebrity Big Brother

Oh God, just one more interview and then it will be over, I tell myself.

Out of the corner of my eye, all I can see are flashing lights and endless TV cameras pointing at me, capturing our every move. We all sit in a line and watch as, one by one, the remaining contestants leave the house to cheers (and the odd pantomime jeer). I sit and think how lucky I am that I managed to escape the boos of the crowd, despite the fact that I hadn't been remotely myself in the house.

You never know what the public will think of you or how the TV execs will edit the footage they get. That's one of the huge risks of going on a reality TV show (I should know!), and even though that's what I did for a living, I was still so nervous – you are a hundred per cent in their hands and you can't control how they make you look. You just have to hope that if you are genuine and don't dig anyone out on purpose, the public will see you are an okay person. Obviously I know what it is like to be on a show like that and how you can be made to look and sometimes it really backfires. I mean, given all the aggro in the house between Jim Davidson and all the women, it could have gone either way for him – all the female fans could have mega lashed out or he could have ended up the popular dark horse – as it turned out that's what happened and he won. To be fair, even Jim was shocked!

I looked down the line at all the other celebs who were already out – it was so great to see Linda Nolan again. She had been so good and lovely to me in the house when I was ill (they all had, to be fair), and I was sorry she got such a hard time when she came out. She was like a mum to me in there when I really needed one. Seeing the footage again, I just wanted to put my arm round her as she looked so gutted and genuinely shocked that she was so hated. To be honest, she was her own worst enemy in the house and I did try to tell her that. She hated Jim so much it started to eat her up and it wasn't until she was gone that we all realized what a downer she'd put on everything. I think it is hard to see reason when you get swept up like that. All you focus on is hurting the other person and I think she genuinely forgot she was on TV.

It went particularly toxic once Jim mentioned stuff which had taken place in Frank Carson's dressing room – that was it and she took it nuclear. Us young ones had no idea what Jim meant or who Frank Carson was, but people like Lionel Blair knew full well what Jim was getting at and we were left in no uncertain terms that it wasn't cool and Jim had well and truly crossed the line. It was such a shame that she let him take over the whole experience for her. As I say, I saw her lovely side and she really, really looked after me when I was in the house and so ill – I was grateful she was there and had my back. Linda made it to one of my fireworks kitchen parties where she turned up with her niece. The girls had her singing her smash hit 'I'm In The Mood For Dancing', she was so much fun.

As for the rest of them, where to start?! You've no idea what they didn't show on TV – Lionel Blair and the sex party, Lee Ryan and his antics. (He is a very strange guy, and that was obvious from the minute he came through the door. I had his card marked from the minute I met him. I couldn't stand him and his 'poor little boy' act.) I don't dislike many people but I really didn't like Lee from the word go and the whole on–off thing with Casey Batchelor and Jasmine Waltz was so draining after a while. I still don't get what the hell they saw in him. It must have been something as there was certainly a lot that went on in that bathroom – trust me, you didn't see the half of it! If you had, the show would have had to be aired after midnight!

Although I am not a prude, in all the time I was on *TOWIE* I would never let them film me in any kind of physical situation with my love interests – even when I was with Joey it took ages for me to feel relaxed. The episode in Series 2 when we kiss in the swimming pool is about as far as I would ever let it go on screen and even that felt like a step too far. I don't know what it is but I have always been like that really. I think it is because my mum always brought us up to have proper self-respect and be ladylike at all times, to stay in control. In the public eye or not, our mum would kill us if we behaved improperly! She always drummed it into us that there is no excuse, ever, for not acting like a lady – and that can mean anything that involves too much swearing, sleeping with a boy too quickly, dressing tarty or drinking too much. She has always told us only we are responsible for our own behaviour and how we come across. I suppose this has been more obvious since *TOWIE* as we have a responsibility to our younger fans who look up to us. Unlike some, I also realized very early on that the press see everything and bad behaviour will always come out eventually. I would never want to let my fans or family down, especially not publicly on the front of a tabloid. It comes home to me big time when I do any kind of signing as the queue is so often made up of nine to sixteen-year-olds and I know they are impressionable and, rightly or wrongly, they look to people like me and Billie who are in the magazines and the public eye for a steer on how to dress and how to behave. They want to know how we do things and that message has to be right and proper. In a world of bad news and questionable role models, I feel very privileged to be seen as doing okay enough for mums to be happy at the thought of their daughter following what I do and taking a lead from my behaviour.

Although I was still unhealthily body obsessed, by the time I went into the house I had tried to take some positive steps to help my self-image. As I mentioned earlier, I had been working closely with Laurie who helped me hone my look into a classier one, enabling me to leave *TOWIE* firmly behind. She taught me about matching colours, fabric, about the right length for skirts and so much more.

The first thing she taught me was to work out what suited my shape and stick to it – experimenting is great but if you find something that works for you, keep it as your fail-safe look. We all need a comfort look that we know works – our Little Black Dress equivalent.

The second thing she was great on was helping to identify my problem area (my arms), but everyone is different – if you have short legs then wear a heel, preferably a nude one, never wear an ankle strap and avoid calf boots that cut you off at the wrong point. If you have big boobs, avoid horizontal stripes, anything too low cut or a belt around your middle and don't squash them down with tops or vests that are too tight. Do wear things nipped in at the waist to show off your top line. If you have wide hips, try not to wear bold prints in skirts or jeans and block colouring can work well too. I am a real girly girl when it comes to my fashion and I've always had a strong sense of what I like, though I have had my fair share of fashion disasters in the early days! I look back at some of my outfits and I am mortified I went out looking like that. Most people have their fashion disaster moments as they are growing up and only have a few photos to remind them – mine are all online! Now, my taste has changed so much. I love pastels and floaty skirts for the summer. I do try and be brave when it comes to mixing and matching but the priority is always comfort, especially if I am having my picture taken – there is nothing worse than seeing people at events and watching them pulling down a skirt that's too short or pulling up a low-cut top. Don't be a fashion victim is my best advice. I know that I am lucky to be able to work with a stylist but we very much work together on my look and I know she would never try and force me into something that wasn't me. I do have classic pieces that look great and have sentimental value too – my favourite is the beautiful Burberry mac that Billie bought me – I will keep it for ever and hand it on to Nelly. It is classic and reminds me of Billie every time I wear it.

Looking good mattered to me but so did how people judged me overall and I hoped *Big Brother* would give me the chance to show what a straightforward and decent person I am. I always want to be a credit to my mum and the way she raised me. That is one of the reasons all the Joey/jungle press upset me so much – the papers were using old topless pictures of me to promote the stories they were either making up or getting from Joey's camp. That meant there were loads of mothers out there who thought I was doing all that again. Don't get me wrong, I'm proud of what I did before I was famous and wouldn't change it, I really wouldn't, but that's not what the fans who follow me now know me for, and when they support me that isn't what mums want their daughters buying into and I understand and respect that. I know I have a responsibility to live the way I preach and I never forget it. My mum has always supported me and Billie in whatever we have done – Billie did the glamour modelling too – and her main thing has always been that we are safe, happy and working hard at whatever we do and doing it well. Also, that we treat others as we wish to be treated and never let ourselves down, that we can look in the mirror at ourselves and be proud. She took such pride in bringing us up the right way – to be kind and stand up for what we believe in. I see it even now with tiny Nelly that she just knows what's right and the way things should be. I am so lucky to have such a great mum and family and I never forget that, and I know that Billie will be exactly the same with Nelly.

But that final night, in my head, as I watched Casey leave the house before me, then from the outside I saw Luisa, Ollie, Dappy & Jim, I tried deep breathing and to keep focussed for this last bit before I was free. I was feeling dizzy and weak and I just wanted to be tucked up on my mum's sofa catching up on *Coronation Street* and drinking a cup of tea. But most of all, I wanted to know why I was feeling so terrible.

The camera pans over to me – I see Emma Willis quizzing Ollie about 'us' and if there will be a romance now we are out. I haven't got a bad word to say about Ollie – he is a sweetheart, even if he was accused of being a bit of a wimp in there. He just wanted to please everyone all the time and I can see that sometimes that made him seem wet but he did genuinely hate rowing, he ran a mile when everything kicked off! But he is a good bloke and was lovely to me. I do think he liked me but there were mixed signals, especially since I have watched some of the show back. I do like to think his feelings for me in there were genuine and not a 'showmance game'. I don't think he is that sort of guy. I felt bad for Ollie, he got a lot of stick for not voicing his opinions in the house, though he did say more than once that he thought I was 'beautiful', which was so lovely to hear. He is like me, very family-orientated and I know his mum means the world to him.

One of the scenes I will always remember is when my mum came into the house during that special 'frozen in time' task. It was by far the most emotional night of the whole series and amongst all the bitching, sneaky sexual stuff in the bathroom and the more open love triangle dramas, it was so lovely to be visited by the people we all missed the most. I just remember the chimes going and my lovely mummy popping through the grandfather clock as we were all forced to remain completely still. I was completely overwhelmed and broke down, though I knew I had to hold it together or lose the task. She came straight over to me and held my face the way she always does when she is trying to reassure me. We know each other so well that I could tell she was worried about me. By then I had lost so much weight and if she was watching every night, she would have been able to see I wasn't myself. I was desperate to talk to her but knew I had to keep silent in order not to throw the task. It was torture and made all the harder knowing that Lee had completely let the side down by answering back to Jasmine when she came in and told him and Casey exactly what she thought.

But Mum knew I wouldn't want a fuss, or any accusation of emotional blackmail for votes – she knew that after everything I had been through, I wanted to do this on my own terms and that it was really important for my self-esteem to know that where I came in the process was down to me and me alone. So she didn't mention my illness on air as I hadn't.

She took her lead from how discreet I was being, and I am so grateful for that. She reassured me that I was doing great and that the outside world were supporting me. I will always remember her words: 'Everyone out there loves you, we miss you so much and you've done us all proud. You look beautiful.' It was the most amazing thing to hear when I knew I wasn't my usual self and worried that people outside hated me for being so boring.

But then it got better when she made a move to talk about Ollie: 'How about Ollie then? He's gorgeous and he's definitely got our seal of approval. I want to carry you out [to] come home with me, my little angel. I can't wait for you to come home.' That was it, we all dissolved. Then she went over to Ollie himself, who already had tears falling down his face, and gave him such a sweet kiss on the cheek! She told him, 'Everyone loves you too. You're doing amazing!'

Ollie's own mum came in after mine and then he really couldn't contain himself. It was so sweet to think of sharing the show with our mums; it will always be one of the most special moments ever, very different from the few times Mum has been on screen during *TOWIE*. I truly never imagined that she would be the one to come into the house as things like that usually mortify her. She hates any kind of attention with a passion, which I can understand. Everyone thinks that I am really confident, but although I am outgoing I can actually be really shy and find the attention difficult sometimes. I said repeatedly to the guys that if I got any visitor at all it would definitely be Billie, not Mum, never in a million years and yet there she was. Billie told me that the *TOWIE* bosses had put stops on her coming in to see me. She had really fought to come in but they wouldn't allow it so it gave Mum no choice and pushed her out of her comfort zone to come into the house and on TV. Mum later told me that there was no way they were keeping her away, that she would have been in there no matter what. She was desperate to see me with her own eyes and not rely on producers telling her that I was fine – I clearly wasn't fine but no one really had any idea how ill I was at that point.

If you look at Mum's face in the house when she is looking over at Ollie and then back at me, I can see a glint in her eye. I think she would have loved something to happen with Ollie if he truly made me happy. I remember when we got out of the show and were doing the PR rounds, Ollie did a big interview for *OK!* magazine with the headline: 'My date with Sam will definitely happen'. He talked about being desperate to 'whisk' me away on a first date and, as he compared me to a cat (which I took as a compliment), he is asked if we have had 'the chat'. This interview must have taken place literally the morning after we got out of the house so the only time we would have been able to speak to each other was at the party, where we were both hanging out with our mums. He was so sweet though with *OK!* when he told them how ill I really had been. God knows how any of them could put up with my constant sickness. Though, as I later thought, there was the hardcore group who spent most of their time in the bathroom trying to have sex and then there was Liz who was hard of hearing and wore an eye mask most of the time!

176

Items on Loan

Library name: Greenisland
Library
User name: Wilson, Donna
(Mrs)

Author: Berlin, Amalie,
Title: Breaking her no-
dating rule
Item ID: C901392586
Date due: 19/12/2016,23:
59
Date charged: 7/11/2016,
11:40

Author: Smith, Sean, 1965-
Title: Kylie
Item ID: C901167751
Date due: 19/12/2016,23:
59
Date charged: 7/11/2016,
5:01

librariesNI

Our families had met over the weeks at Elstree during *CBB*. Ollie was always so lovely about me in interviews: 'She's just an absolute sweetheart. She's lovely and she's not like other reality stars. She's very down to earth, very sweet. She isn't fame-hungry.' I don't know what it was but there just wasn't the 'fizz' there, if that makes sense? I think that it is a classic case of being thrown together in a suffocating environment like the *Big Brother* house. We probably had the most in common with each other given what we did for a living and obviously what goes with that is an understanding of how reality TV works for and against you. I was ill and vulnerable and he was lovely and had no side.

Back there, on eviction night, I smile as the camera comes back to me and blush a bit as Emma asks Ollie about his feelings for me. But to be honest, I am not really in the zone. I feel so bad, I don't really recognize myself and I just want this all to be over. It's been an incredible experience but I feel an overwhelming sadness that I wasn't well enough to really enjoy it and I am so worried about how boring I must have seemed or, worse, aloof. When I came out I saw an article in which the *Sunday People* described me as the most boring woman in the UK. Thanks guys. I was so determined not to whinge and moan that I just sort of shut down and withdrew into myself, like self-preservation, but that can also seem like you can't be bothered and aren't interested in what is going on around you, which couldn't be further from the truth. If I let my guard down and allowed my brain to engage with how dreadful I really felt, I knew there was no way I would get through the eviction evening and also the following day of back-to-back press. I had to keep it together for just a few more hours. That's all it would take before I could relax.

People didn't see the real me in there – I mean, I am laid-back and all, but never like that. I felt barely conscious some of the time. The truth is that for most of my time in the house, I could barely lift my head off the pillow. I couldn't keep anything down for three of the four weeks I was in there, my face exploded in a mass of painful boils, I couldn't stand the bright lights that never seemed to go off, I was in pain all over and I just wanted my mum. Everyone else (apart from Liz!) was drunk all the time and having a merry and mad time, really letting go, and I had two hospital visits during my time on the show, though they were never discussed. After the first few days, it got so bad I had to eat special meals on my own in the diary room. They gave me lots of creamy foods to try to smooth the flare-ups as they kept telling me it was IBS or a similar inflammation. I found out later the public had seen none of this, no wonder they thought I was boring. Katie Price won the latest *CBB* series and had a similar experience of being ill in the house. Like me she fought it and stayed in to win which was amazing.

On the actual eviction night when I left the house, there was no great elated feeling really as I knew I was still on camera. As I sat amongst everyone, watching Jim being crowned the champion, there was only one thing on my mind. I just wanted to know what was wrong with me and if I was going to be okay. The public had no idea that I was so poorly. Every effort was taken to play it down and keep it from the voters. I didn't disagree with that strategy either; I mean, there is nothing worse than watching a celeb on a reality TV show who spends the whole time moaning about illness. I certainly didn't want to be that person. We have all sat at home and watched people struggle with the eating tasks in the jungle or lose it a bit in the *Celebrity Big Brother* house, and then wonder why on earth these people agreed to the show if they weren't prepared to get stuck in. I totally appreciate it doesn't make for good viewing. That said, two days after the show was over, I was on *This Morning* with the rest of the finalists and I was told by Eamonn Holmes that I had been boring. As we looked over the footage from the house and some of our best bits (which did involve a lot of sexy behaviour on the part of the others) Eamonn said to me: 'Ahh, come on, Sam, where WERE you during all this? You didn't drink, you didn't get up to much.' I remember smiling and trying to be as polite as possible as I said my stock answer of the day, 'Well, what you all didn't see was how poorly I was in there.'

I think that the outside world only heard that there was something wrong when Liz Jones came out of the house. That's when Adam says he really realized the seriousness of what was going on with me. I was up for nomination with her and Jim, but she got evicted – I actually think she was relieved to go. She found it so hard in there – she is partially deaf and she didn't really fit in as she isn't easy-going and has so many hang-ups it's unreal really. I don't know how she has got through life and ever worked with another person! She is so hard on herself, when she got out she told Emma Willis that she had 'post-traumatic stress'! She struggled massively with how dirty communal living can make a house, and she is clearly a neat freak in real life (so am I, though I was too ill to really do anything about it). I spent a lot of time looking after Liz, doing her hair and letting her borrow my clothes. She was such a sweet lady.

I think she liked us in the end. She said people would be surprised that we had 'depth' and her being cuffed to Dappy was hilarious viewing in itself. But she is partial to stirring up the odd headline to suit herself, which came across in how split she was when she was discussing me. On the one hand, she tried to make out that I had an agenda and that I was 'trying hard to look sexy for the cameras' by doing things like showering in a bikini with the main door open deliberately: 'I think Sam just wants everyone to like her. She has never rowed with anyone. Her and Ollie's careers are reality TV and doing personal appearances so they need people to like them. I'd love to see her really explode and lose her rag – but she is very controlled.' She then goes on to stick up for me a bit by saying that the fans had no idea how ill I had been: 'Sam has been accused of being quiet and boring but there is a reason. She has been ill for two weeks. Some days she was so bad they let her stay in bed because she was really sick. She has a virus. It hasn't helped her time in the house. I gather none of this has been shown and people don't know.'

So, on the one hand, I was attention-seeking and trying really hard to get the camera on me and, on the other, I was so ill I was left to stay in bed and therefore so boring no one wanted to film me! I know there were those outside who thought there was a game plan, that I knew 'good' people win and so was trying to be one of the 'quiet' ones who slipped under the radar and didn't offend and so made it to the final. Truth be told, even if that was the plan (and it wasn't!) I wouldn't have had the energy to execute it.

What has never really made that much sense to me is why they didn't show how ill I was, especially as nothing was really off-limits for a show that fed off the contestants' drama. I mean, obviously the first thing I was going to do when I got out of the house was explain why I hadn't been myself and that would involve telling people how ill I had been. Don't get me wrong, I had no wish to go into detail about the sickness and diarrhoea and the boils all over my face. I was lying on the floor sobbing and they were all helping me up to the diary room, practically carrying me, as I didn't have the strength to walk up there. I spent a full two days in bed without moving and I will say that I couldn't have been with a better bunch of people in terms of being looked after – I hadn't known any of them before I went into the house and they looked after me with such genuine kindness, especially after I got back from the hospital each time.

Anyway, ill or not, it didn't affect my ability to be amused by the characters in there! It was such a random mix of people and there was so much bad behaviour that didn't even get hinted at, let alone shown. There are a few who stand out for me; one of them has to be Lionel – who knew he had such a hilarious side? Though he did have a terrible temper. He rowed with people and, in my mind, could be a bit gossipy. We were all gobsmacked when he called Luisa a 'self-centred bitch' after he goaded her into breaking the rules and then denied it. But I really like Lionel, he was like a granddad figure, we got on really well and he was really sweet to me.

I love Luisa so much. She is so straight down the line, even if the truth isn't what you want to hear, you get it from her anyway. She just calls it how it is and that is so refreshing. She gave as good as she got and shut him up! Her and Lionel did patch it up, but that was because she was prepared to be the bigger person and I admired her for that. I am not sure I could have coped with him ranting at me like that. From the *CBB* experience Luisa Zissman became a true friend. It's funny that at the start I didn't see it, but as we went on I really got to love her and we have been in touch every day since. I took Billie and Nelly round to Luisa's recently and we had a spa day together, which was so lovely. Luisa's daughter Dixie is so cute and adores Nelly.

I did think Lionel was quite funny about Jasmine, who clearly got on his nerves from the beginning – although he should have been me and been handcuffed to her! She got hammered on the launch night and, to be honest, was just a nightmare. It was dreadful being stuck to her – people who are drunker than you are a nightmare at the best of times, but being cuffed to them on a reality TV show where your every move is monitored is horrendous. It took every ounce of patience I had, and I also knew that I would be judged on how I handled her and the situation. Thankfully I wasn't feeling ill at that point and so just decided to look after her like I would any mate who had drunk too much after a night out at Sugar Hut! I felt the best thing I could do for her was get her to bed and out of trouble, but Jasmine was having none of it and tried to literally drag me for a cigarette and, in the process, began rolling around on the floor. Lionel was cuffed to Ollie and didn't try to hide his disgust: 'I don't like her being like that. I've got a daughter and she would never behave like that. It's awful.' That's when I first got an idea of what a nice guy and diplomat Ollie was. Even though Jasmine was being a total nutter, his response was characteristically sweet: 'She was brought up in Vegas and that's a very different world.'

Lionel definitely had it in for Casey in his exit interview and accused her of keeping the drama going with Lee, not because she liked him but because she knew it guaranteed her airtime. I personally never thought that about Casey. I always thought part of what wound me up so much in there about Lee was the fact that both those girls genuinely loved him, and he knew it and STILL behaved so terribly. Lionel and Ollie were very sweet together, I must say, and I know that Lionel was supporting one of us to win.

I saw when I got out though, how shocked some people had been at his behaviour during the 'adults only' show – it was such a random task! Me, Luisa, Jasmine, Lee, Ollie and Lionel all dressed up in a PVC combo of basques and jackets (and budgie smugglers in Lee's case), and had to put on a raunchy burlesque show. Lionel, who had previously despaired at the sexy behaviour of some contestants, started shouting into the camera: 'Suck my ****!' Seriously, who knew that it would end up with Lionel the raunchy star! To be fair, things got very out of hand very quickly as the *CBB* bosses actively encouraged bad behaviour – we were definitely briefed to use terrible language and they were cheering everyone on as things got hot and heavy – they even nicknamed the room where we were filming the party the 'sex dungeon'. Lionel said some unspeakable things which I wouldn't ever dream of printing in my book, it would make your hairs curl! They were extremely pleased when Jasmine started shouting at Lee: 'I love your boner!' She was out of control and a gift to a reality TV show. Thinking back on it they definitely pulled off a ratings winner. I was aware I had to join in so I didn't look like I was being a disapproving prude but I think that was the hardest task for me. I was so ill and had zero energy and things like that make me really uncomfortable – I just can't help it. Although it was very entertaining I was so out of my comfort zone! But we did manage to have fun, not least watching them all get so out of control. I laugh a lot when I'm nervous and I definitely got the giggles on that task.

And then there was Lee – once me and Jasmine were uncuffed, that was the beginning of him chasing her and trying to cause as much havoc as possible. I won't lie, I found their displays and sexiness a bit cringe – it was so against how I thought people should behave on TV and I just imagined Mum and Billie's faces if I even thought about behaving like

Going into the *Celebrity Big Brother* house – I was really nervous but so excited at the same time.

Being in the house was a lot of fun and I made some great friends in there, like Luisa Zissman (*left*).

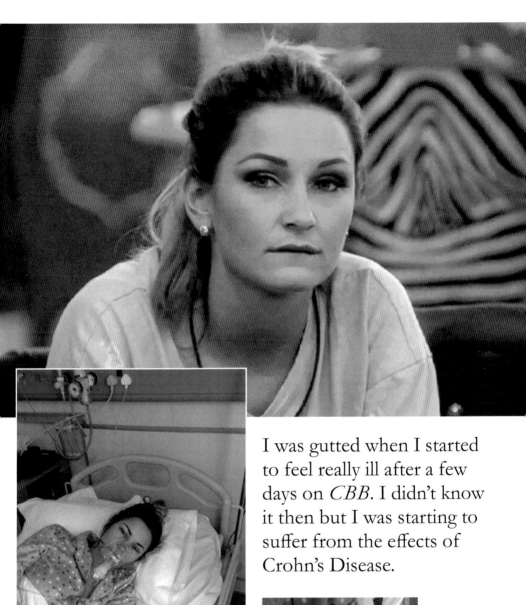

I was gutted when I started to feel really ill after a few days on *CBB*. I didn't know it then but I was starting to suffer from the effects of Crohn's Disease.

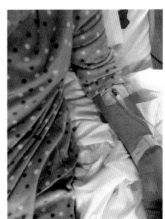

After meeting on *TOWIE*, Joey and I have
had a really roller coaster relationship on
and off screen. This was our first date after
we got back together last year.

These are a few pics from my
personal archive when Joey and I
were at one of our happiest points.

In Cape Town.

Getting engaged was such a big moment for me and I was devastated when we decided to call it off.

I now feel better than ever. I've got my health,
my happiness and my confidence back.

Flashing some
serious side boob
at the National
Television Awards!

All dressed up for
the premiere of
The Hunger Games:
Mockingjay.

that on TV! I would die of embarrassment! I can't emphasize enough how much was NOT shown on TV when it came to the sexy bits. Jasmine hinted at it when she left the show and gave an interview detailing how 'aroused' they were by each other and that they may even have had sex in the house. We all looked on in slight horror as they sucked each other's toes, snogged like mad, and kept slipping off to the bit of the bathroom without the cameras during the spaceship task – things got very steamy and out of hand. As she told the *Daily Star*: 'We kissed and made out and did stuff – but we turned on the taps so people wouldn't hear us. We wanted privacy. We got very close. We didn't want people hearing our business. It was the only place we could go without the cameras on us.' She told us repeatedly in the house that he was always 'aroused, always turned on'. She boasted: 'We did everything we wanted to do in there'.

Her take on Casey was obviously very one-sided, for her Casey had to be a bunny boiler. Although it is very different, I would say that after all the off and on with Joey, where he was telling me one thing off camera and then doing another on camera, I can totally sympathize with Casey for having her head messed with. There is nothing worse than being led on and not knowing where you stand – as I found out it can be enough to drive you slightly mad. That said, I would have loved her to have had a bit more self-respect. No guy is worth all that public angst, especially not Lee Ryan!

I think Lee had such a lucky escape leaving the house the way he did as the crowd would have destroyed him if he'd had to face them by going out the front way, but he didn't escape the wrath of Casey's mum when she came into the house for the 'frozen in time' task. She had some proper blunt words for her little girl: 'Listen to me carefully. Keep away from Lee. Honestly, darling, he tells you one thing and then behind your back he tells housemates other things. And when he's in the diary room he says you get on his t**s and you won't leave him alone. He's mugged you off, darling, he's mugged you off.' Literally the best phrase ever! Properly brilliant and props to her. I wouldn't want to mess with her and would have loved to have seen Lee's face whilst she was in there ratting him out, but I was sort of facing the other way. I will confess though that I have watched it back and it makes me cringe at the thought of being Lee!

I loved her mum for coming in and having her girl's back like that. I know my mum would have done the same if it were me and I had total respect for her sticking up for Casey. I was trying so hard not to smile or cheer! It has to be one of my favourite moments, but the most awkward moment had to be when Jasmine came back in. Oh my God, it was so awful. To be fair, having had people talking about Joey and Amy in the jungle, I had an idea of how difficult it might have been, although this was obviously far more upsetting as he had been with Jasmine when she was evicted and, as far as she was concerned, they were a proper couple (or as much of one as you can be on a reality TV show where you are locked up together!). Yet, as she said to Casey when she came in: 'As soon as my back was turned, as soon as I left you found [the] prime opportunity to throw yourself at him. And it is quite embarrassing actually . . . You intentionally and deliberately went out to hurt me . . . You saw us together . . . and yet . . . putting your t**s in his face . . . and how you woke up so horny.' She went on to point out that, as a girl's girl, she was coming across really badly and as a 'bunny boiler'. I thought that she was a bit cruel to Casey actually, as there is nothing worse than being locked in there and worrying about what people on the outside are saying and how you are being portrayed when you can do absolutely nothing about it. It felt unnecessarily harsh and personal, though I guess I wasn't the one having to watch someone I thought was my boyfriend sharing a bed with my arch rival. Nothing so unhinged as a woman scorned – they actually both showed that in the way they behaved. There was certainly no such thing as 'girl power' or the sisterhood with those two! When Lee left the house he and Jasmin went about shooting magazine covers and having pictures taken on holiday in Thailand. Weeks later they split.

But whatever other people's issues in there, my experience of the other contestants was a good one. I have looked back on some past shows and line-ups and realize that I had a very easy ride indeed. There wasn't anyone evil in there (and I am not sure I could have coped with George Galloway imitating a cat!). It was just as well that if I was to go in there and get sick, I did it with a kind bunch. They were genuinely so worried about me. I was worried about myself if the truth be told. Whilst I was in there I concentrated on how I was coming across and not looking like a moaner, but once I was out and my mum was back in charge, it was time to find out what was going on. I got out of the house and then had the wrap party to get through. I couldn't eat or drink and I remember standing by the bar with Adam, contemplating if I needed the loo for the millionth time after a simple sip of water. My Mum and Aunty Libby had come along and were incredibly concerned about how I was doing. My stomach cramps were intolerable – I was doubled up – but being there was part of my contract. I was clinging on to the side of the bar, with everyone telling me how awful I looked.

Style.com

Looking back on the show, it wasn't exactly me at my fashionable best, especially when I was so ill. Glamour was the last thing on my mind. However, when I am feeling like going for it in the fashion stakes, here are my top tips:

- Legs or boobs, never both on show – the ultimate faux pas – always keep it classy.

- Don't be a fashion slave – not everything you see in a magazine will suit you. Most of us aren't six foot two with legs up to our armpits! Remember, those girls do it for a living and being thin is their job. We all have looks that suit us and there is something out there for everyone.

- Aside from my Very.co.uk lines that I have and I love wearing, I am a great believer in mixing and matching. A classic and well-finished pair of trousers or skirt that cost that little bit more can be easily teamed with an on-trend top to create the ultimate outfit.

- Every girl needs a great pair of jeans that skim the thighs and hug the bum – a must-have. This is along with the ultimate pencil skirt with split up the back (never the front or side), a classic white shirt, navy or black blazer, cigarette pants and an expensive pair of black leather heels. This is your staple mix and can be added to and enhanced.

- I like to get my hair done professionally before I go out, but how I wear it will all depend on my outfit. If I am going to a posh function in a floor length gown, I will wear my hair up, but if it is daytime and my outfit is casual or simple, then I will give my hair lots of volume.

- Some of my favourite high street stores include: River Island, Topshop, Hennes, Cos, ASOS, Miss Selfridge, Zara and Mango. They are all great for trend fashion items but, most of all, for well-priced shoes and hand-bags. I love online fashion and I am delighted to be working with the Shop Direct Group and Very.co.uk. I have my own apparel collections which do really well, as well as swimwear which I am so excited about.

10

Health and Wealth

Living with Crohn's Disease

had mixed feelings about getting out of the house – despite being ill I'd had the experience of a lifetime, but now I was so weak and drained and still had a lot of PR to do. I was well aware of my obligations and didn't want to let anyone down.

After the wrap party, I headed to the Village Hotel in Watford for the night. But the next day there was little time to rest. The press I was contracted to do had to take place twenty-four hours after I left the house – it included a gruelling day of radio, TV and print interviews and, most worryingly, a photo shoot of me in a bikini or lingerie (to be honest, I had no idea why, given it was February, but there you go). I always do what I am asked to and what I am supposed to – I am no diva on shoots, not precious about anything, will try any clothes, make-up or new hair look, but I just couldn't face this shoot. I had showered that morning and it was the first time I had taken a look at myself naked since going into the house. There had obviously been no privacy and, despite what Liz Jones reckoned about me prancing around in my bikini, I was certainly no exhibitionist (unlike Jasmine who had to be persuaded to actually wear any clothes!). I knew I had lost weight but not even I could tell I was nearly three stone lighter than before I went into the house. What I saw in the mirror, standing in my mum's bathroom, made me gasp in horror – my hip bones jutted out so far and were so sharp at the top I thought they might cut through my knicker elastic. It was like they had been sharpened with a nail file. I was scared. I remember layering up for the day of press ahead: there was little I could do about my razor-sharp cheekbones, so I slapped on the foundation and tried to strategically place the blusher so it didn't accentuate the new-found bone lines too much, and kept my hair loose so that I could cover my face. Despite what the papers went on to say, I didn't enjoy emphasizing my weight loss and I wasn't 'proud of all my hard work'. I felt dreadful, no two ways about it, even if it did make good copy.

I had agreed to an interview and photo shoot with a leading national newspaper, an 'exclusive' agreed with the *Celebrity Big Brother* producers that talked about my time in the house – all the finalists had one lined up. Part of the agreement was this exclusive photo shoot, and they wanted sexy pictures. Anyway, Adam politely explained that I was extremely unwell and, although I was more than determined to fulfil my press obligations today, the photo shoot would be a little harder given my condition. He told them that I had been struck down with something in the house, that I was very poorly and would be going to seek medical help when the press day was over. He went on to explain that I couldn't eat or drink, that I was constantly shivering and that I had lost a worrying amount of weight. Not only did I feel awful but, to be honest, I looked awful and the weight loss was breathtaking. I obviously didn't want to be seen or photographed looking like that, but I also genuinely didn't want my young fans to see me like that and think that I was parading that kind of body as something to aspire to. I felt dangerously ill but I also looked it too and the last thing I wanted was to be irresponsible. I also just didn't really fancy taking my clothes off and trying to keep up the banter required at a shoot like that – I didn't have the energy. I wanted to do my press but, if I wasn't well enough, I didn't want any bad press.

Throughout the photo call with with the other *CBB* contestants, all the photographers did was ask about my weight loss and try to force me and Ollie to stand next to each other, touching, holding hands, which wasn't what either of us wanted so we tried to avoid it.

We got through the rest of the day just about and I headed back to Mum's. I was teary, exhausted and still so worried about myself. I was so relieved that we were going for some tests the following day. That said, I couldn't wait for my mum to bundle me up and look after me. I remember her lovely cosy house being so welcoming. She wrapped me up in blankets and duvets and got me into bed but, no matter what I did or how hot they tried to make me, I couldn't stop shivering. My teeth were chattering and I was covered in goosebumps; it wasn't right – like flu but a million times worse. Nothing helped and I could see that everyone was desperately worried. I tried to sleep that night, so happy to be in my childhood bed with my mummy next door – and with lights that went out and not being surrounded by random peoples' breathing and snoring! It felt weird but so, so good.

The next morning I was up to do the stint on *This Morning* with the other finalists. Adam picked me up at 7 a.m. He said I looked grey and exhausted and I know my mum didn't want me going anywhere in that state: I hadn't slept and I still couldn't keep a thing down. She gave me a look as I put my seat belt on in the front of Adam's car – but she also knew I would fulfil my obligations, no matter what. I had signed up to this and wanted to see it through. It was also weekly magazine day and Adam had a pile to go through. The first thing that caught my eye was the headline: 'Sam Faiers: My Cancer Scare'. That was not what I wanted – the magazines speculating before I even knew what was happening myself.

That afternoon, Lauren my PR arranged for me to go to Freedomhealth, another of her clients, for a whole host of tests. I saw a fantastic doctor there, who was really thorough with everything. We sneaked in without being seen, though by the time we had been there twenty minutes, there was a gaggle of photographers out the front, shouting my name and trying to get info. I stayed there for ages for so many tests and, as I was waiting in a room upstairs, I suddenly collapsed. The staff were amazing and checked me over before making me comfortable and then worked to hatch a plan to get me out and to another hospital for admission, rehydration and rest. By this point, there were loads of paps now clicking away at the front of the building, so I was bundled up and ushered out of the back exit, away from lenses, and able to get to a Harley Street hospital where I would stay for a couple of nights.

Straight away they put lots of intravenous lines in and started to pump me full of the nutrients and liquids that I had been so horrendously lacking. I was chronically dehydrated and weak. I stayed put and rested for a few days with Mum, Billie and friends by my side. I know my mum was terrified, I could see it in her eyes, but she is so good at the brave face – she kept her voice upbeat and her tone light, and kept talking about when I got home and how well I was doing. But I knew she was scared that they still didn't know what was wrong or how to fix it.

As I had been taken in suddenly I had nothing with me and I remember Adam going off from Harley Street to Oxford Street to buy supplies – he came back armed with pyjamas, dressing gowns, slippers, magazines – you name it, he had thought of it. It is weird how when you are in a hospital bed all sorts of thoughts fly around your head as you have far too much time on your hands, and all I could think about was the time when Joey was in the jungle and I lost the plot. I remembered how difficult I had been: not eating, over-exercising, paranoid and angry at the world. Once I had some perspective, I knew that you only give your nearest and dearest grief because you feel secure. Believe me, I know that I was challenging for everyone, but lying in that hospital bed I really did work out what mattered and it was just getting out of there and knowing what I needed to do in order to get better.

My immune system was shot to bits and I was picking up every cold and cough going. I had over twelve blood tests, a colonoscopy, CT scans and ultrasounds, and my blood sugar levels were checked (they thought I might have anaemia) – you name it, I was tested for it and still no one knew anything. I was on a drip for rehydration for thirty-five hours. My bowels were epically swollen and my intestines enlarged, and the stomach cramps were intolerable. I had lost a worrying amount of weight, and I was riddled with ulcers and chronic pain. I knew from the outset that whatever it was the doctors could treat it – they were clear about that so, unlike a lot of the magazines said, I did not fear I was going to die there and then. I just felt terrible and wanted to know why.

I knew that, given it was treatable, if I was lucky the only thing I would have to do was to make some changes to my diet. For a long time the doctors thought it was a nasty virus. The immediate and big weight loss was down to loss of appetite. Anyone who is ill knows what that is like – you can't face anything – and I just felt constantly full up, obviously due to the inflammation and liquid retention in my stomach area. It was such a weird feeling – unlike before, when I was trying to get slim, when I had been delighted with every pound I lost and I'd rejoiced when I stood on the scales and saw movement in the downward direction. Now I hated how slim I was because I knew it was a sign of ill health. I also hated seeing my mum so worried about me.

Obviously my close friends and family knew and I had deliberately told the *TOWIE* girls like Gemma, Jess and

Ferne to stay away from the hospital as I didn't want the papers writing stories and catching them off guard for out-of-context comments. We let *TOWIE* know that I was on bed rest and would keep them updated about any changes and also when they might expect me back for filming.

My head was all over the place – after all that time around strangers in a public house covered in cameras and sleeping in a weird bed, I just wanted my family. I didn't want any drama, anything to do with the show or any accusations of using it for post-house PR. I know that sounds cynical, but you do get used to the upsetting press and have to be pre-pared. I had been lucky so far but you can never take it for granted. I also wanted to get my own head around it before I dealt with the tears and the questions of others. I didn't even know what I thought at that point but, however it panned out, I knew that significant changes needed to be made and that life would never be the same again. I was also aware that I needed to get my medical facts straight for when I commu-nicated it to the fans, anything medical like that isn't like recommending a nail varnish or blusher, it's really serious and, again, I was very aware of the responsibility.

That is quite a moment, to sit with a doctor and get the diagnosis of Crohn's Disease. No one can ever really under-stand unless they have been there, and I needed to process it as I knew that Mum and Billie would be taking their lead from me and that I needed to be strong. It was such an awful and stressful time.

It was a huge relief though to finally be diagnosed and my

attitude right from the start was: 'Fine, it isn't ideal, but it also isn't terminal. Plenty of people hear and deal with much worse and, as long as I know what I am dealing with, I can control it.' My poor mum and Billie took it much harder than me. There were lots of tears and lots of my mum feeling helpless and desperate to take my place and take the pain. You only have to watch back that scene filmed for *TOWIE* in my living room just after I was diagnosed to see how emotional she was, but I was adamant that, once I knew what was what, it was onwards and upwards. Also, I don't think I appreciated how weak and frail I appeared to the onlooker. It was hard for Mum too to see me so physically fragile, to know she couldn't do anything to help make me better. Billie says it all the time now when she looks at Nelly, how awful it would be not to be able to just make it all better for her if something was wrong.

All I wanted was to get well and get back to work, though Adam and my family were really concerned I didn't overdo it and were strict with me. But I was desperate for 'business as usual' and that also meant filming *TOWIE*. I rested up and did one tweet of a picture showing the drip in my arm. It wasn't to be deliberately dramatic or provocative, as some papers said – it was to say hi to the fans and let them know I was okay. There were lots of direct messages, tweets and emails to Adam's office asking where I had gone and if I was okay. The last pictures of me had been in the *Sun*, walking in Brentwood and looking so tiny that there had been loads of speculation when I went off Twitter for a few days. In the old days, your PR would have put out a formal press release if their client was ill, but in the age of Twitter there is no more effective medium for reaching the fans, especially if you have a fair few followers.

The practicalities of the illness kicked in straight away. I was thankful we had taken out health insurance with Minnies for the directors – my whole treatment after my diagnosis was amazing and I couldn't have asked for better care every step of the way. It was faultless. Every little detail was explained to me, and Mum and I were talked through everything I needed to know and a whole lot more. Before I went home I was told that I needed a liquid-only diet for six weeks to reset my bowel and re-educate it. They were also clear that I will have to be on the lookout for relapses for the rest of my life. I was told that I could face surgery if one of those relapses was too severe, and that will always be the case, which is why it is so important to keep on top of everything and be alert to even the smallest symptoms that can take hold in a flash. At the point I was in hospital and being diagnosed, the ulcers were so bad that it was impossible to really assess the situation properly until the swelling had subsided with the help of full-on medication. I was prescribed six nutrient shakes a day filled with liquids, protein and carbohydrates. I didn't even allow myself to dread this new way of life or to think about missing my usual treats and snacks. All that mattered was getting back on my feet and learning to live with my new situation.

I was proud of my upbeat attitude, but that is very much what I am like when the chips are down – it is all about positive thinking. The very last thing I wanted was pity. I just wanted to learn about it, learn about the triggers and get to grips with living with it – I didn't see it as brave, more just being practical about the situation I was in. They had diagnosed me and I would deal with it and my lovely mummy was looking after me so I knew I wasn't on my own.

What didn't help was that people had started to notice my weight loss. If you read some papers I had lost over half of my body weight! Not only did it upset my mum but I was aware of my responsibility – before I got ill I had lost quite a bit of weight, then I upped the exercise and diet regime as I wanted to look good in the *CBB* house, then I got ill and lost a ton more. I didn't want girls out there thinking that any of this recent weight loss was deliberate or that, because it had been going on for a while, it was all part of a plan that I was happy about deep down.

So I went home to Mum's and rested up, got myself together and waited until I was strong enough to get back out there, and it actually wasn't as long as I thought it would be before I felt like myself again. The first step was seeing people again, mainly from the show. Adam had been in touch with the producers about my condition so they weren't reading about it in the papers, but also so they could think about my storylines and how to spin them until I was ready to return. But first I had a revolving door of visitors and I was so happy to see them. People close to me on the show were shocked when they saw me in real life, after I had left the *Big Brother* house. There were definitely tears. I think I looked so different and weak, and that isn't me – I'm not really an 'ill' person. I was like the Queen sitting on Mummy's sofa drinking tea, watching *Friends*, and receiving all my visitors. I know she loved having her baby home and it gave her a chance to catch up with everyone.

It is funny when you are ill, people either step up and show you the love or they disappoint you. I think it is a real mark of character how they behave and I will certainly never forget the ones who didn't bother to step up and make an effort. I had been so preoccupied by my new routine, I hadn't thought of Joey much, and I told myself that was a very good thing indeed. This was my new life now, with things I needed to process; this was the new me. So, of course, it was around this time that Joey got back in touch. Out of the blue I got a text from him. It happened to be a day when I was at my lowest. I remember that beep coming through and a message popping up:

Hiya, I read you are unwell. I hope you're okay, love Joey x

I felt so much better just hearing from him. It might be a cliché but it is true: being ill makes you appreciate so much more what you have, and it was like that for us both. Suddenly it didn't matter what had gone on before: what was happening there and then was so scary – for me that I couldn't control what was happening, and for Joey that he worried he would lose me. But in an effort not to get over-excited at that point, I simply replied:

Hi. Yeah, I have been really poorly. I'm at my mum's now, resting all week. Lovely to hear from you. Love Sam x

We had a bit more back and forth – I wished him luck for his show, *Educating Joey Essex*, he asked me to pass on his congrats to Billie and Greg, who had announced they were having a baby girl (our Nelly-Noo). It was all cautiously polite but I was delighted to be back in touch. Filming for the show had started and I knew mutual friends were feeding back that I looked awful and that he would be asking Tom and Diags (who, to be fair, were really sweet to me). It made me happy to think that he was worried about me and asking after me, that he was being protective even after everything – there it was, that connection again.

The team at *TOWIE* were very good – I had made it clear before I went off to *CBB* that this was not the end of my time on the show. No way did I want to leave by just disappearing for a one-off show on another channel with no explanation, and actually the clever way they dealt with my absence has allowed people like Gemma to do the jungle and come back. I think they would agree they were very keen for me to stay and would have done anything to make that happen – they were clear they were happy for me to do and endorse *CBB* as long as I came back afterwards, which I did. The producers used to be so strict about it – in Harry and Amy's day if you wanted to try something else you were out, no questions asked – just look at Mark Wright, it was the same for him. But they have realized that the way to keep the old-time favourites happy is to try to be as accommodating as possible. I don't mean taking the piss and going with every channel available. I just mean appreciating that there are lots of fun things out there for young people who are in the public eye, and that, like in any relationship, if you treat people well, they want to come back. And, more importantly, the viewers will keep tuning in.

Adam says that deep down I had wanted to leave the show back as early as Series 7 as I wasn't happy with some of the storylines or how much time it took away from my other projects. It was impossible to plan anything – any press days or shoots for Minnies, any meetings in London – as I had to be available and near, almost like being on call. I knew that with the fragrance and the clothing range coming up it would become trickier and trickier. Adam had so much to handle now with me – on top of all the other stuff he now had hundreds of emails a day from people with Crohn's, who said someone in the public eye talking about it had helped or had given them the courage to seek help and get advice rather than suffer in pain. That will always mean a lot to me and that's why, after I left the house and was officially diagnosed, one of the first things I did was agree to an interview with *This Morning* and Dr Chris Steele. It is important to raise awareness whenever you can and I learn something new every day about the disease – and that can only be a good thing.

The producers were very cautious about my return. They limited the number of hours of filming according to my doctor's instructions and were very good when I was too ill to film, which was quite often in those first few weeks as my body adjusted first to the medication and then the change of diet. It was like a full-body meltdown as I took all the medication and cut things out of my daily diet – it took a lot of getting used to. The liquid-only diet lasted over six weeks and once it was over then a very plain eating plan was introduced: white rice, potatoes, chicken, fish, nothing too full of flavour or spice. I had to give up wine – I felt horrific afterwards if I even had one glass (must be the acid) and now I just drink G&Ts, which means I drink far less. I have to avoid acidic foods like tomatoes, curries and fried foods – they give me an instant flare-up. Red meat is also a no-go, as it is too hard to digest. My biggest treat used to be popcorn (mainly as it is fairly healthy with very few calories) but that had to go, as did high-fibre foods like cereal. My new diet plan was eating little and often – going for long periods without food is suicide when it comes to flare-ups. I learned a lot through my research on forums, what to do and what to avoid. Obviously everyone has a different body so what works can vary from person to person. If you do have Crohn's or a similar inflammatory condition, it may be a good idea to do your own research into what works for you.

There was a shoot for the start of Series 11, which was just after I came out of the house, and I could feel the cast looking at me like they didn't recognize me. Gemma being Gemma was outspoken enough to tell me I looked terrible (in a funny way!) and I think for the first time people could see that there was genuinely something scary wrong. The producers definitely looked after me. It was so weird seeing my body have this meltdown – before I went into the *Celebrity Big Brother* house I had been training hard and worked up lots of muscle definition, but it had all gone as the weight fell off and what was left was just this mass of empty skin – I have never seen anything like it. My arms and legs were so weak I frequently had to sit down and rest just waiting to have my photos done. It was so unlike me. I knew it would take time to get back to normal.

Later, once the six-week food ban was up and I had become used to plain and mainly whole foods again, I looked to overhaul my diet in a more permanent way – breakfast became a poached egg on granary bread or porridge, with a small bit of fruit mid-morning, lunch was a salad or a wrap with chicken or tuna, and supper was something light to be eaten before 8 p.m. My new rule was not to eat anything too big in one go that would stretch or put any pressure on the stomach. I knew things could change from day to day – just five days into the *CBB* show I was hot, plagued with dreadful stomach cramps if I ate or drank anything, and throwing up immediately. Now, the new diet provided instant relief and I have never looked back. Sometimes it is tempting to just slack it off and indulge, but it is true when people say it is never worth feeling so dreadful the next day. (It has also meant far fewer hangovers!).

My friends rallied round and were discreet as they knew I didn't want it all over the papers, especially as there were now lots of stories questioning how and why I got the disease, with theories swaying between it being genetic or triggered by viruses, stress or dietary issues. The press were particularly interested as a new series of *TOWIE* was due to start and there was the usual PR circus going on. I didn't really do any interviews, so they started to try to ask the other cast members lots of questions. I remember Jess and Arg being at a press conference for the *Daily Mirror* and being asked a series of questions about what I was eating and my weight. Jess was great. Her answer was: 'It's not really our business to divulge into it but she's okay, I think.'

I loved her for having my back like that as she knew I was struggling a bit with my new dietary regime. She was also great at sticking up for me when it came to my appearance on *CBB*: 'I watched her and it's a shame you didn't get to see more of her because she was really, really ill in that house and I think she did amazing to stay in there for what she did.' Bless Jess for saying that.

Back on the show, I knew we had to address the issue but I didn't want it to be all sad and depressing with everyone wailing around me. I was careful with myself and actually took the decision to miss out on a lot of the fun stuff in Series 11, which was a shame but I knew my health came first. So I missed Mario's big birthday bash, though I did pull it together enough to go to a party at Nu Bar for Billie and Greg's baby reveal. I remember being so cold it was horrible. That wiped me out for days afterwards and, though I had a great time, I regretted it as I knew I had pushed myself too far. Billie had a brilliant idea for a party that wouldn't involve long hours filming in a club, surrounded by food I couldn't eat as I was still in my six-week food ban, or by booze and drunk people, and that was a get-well shake party! It was so sweet and we all sat around tasting various shakes that I had to drink (the girls thought they were disgusting!) and had our hair in rollers so it felt like a proper scene from the olden days. It still managed to be the same old drama though, thanks to the Ferne and Frank Major storyline and the aftermath of Mario's party where it had all kicked off. It sounded mental. Before the shake party, when me and Billie were shopping for ingredients, we 'bumped into' Charlie in the supermarket and that was doubly awkward as he launched into a whole description of what was happening between him, Ferne and Frank, and then in the next episode he and Frank came face to face in a bar. This series was full of high drama all round, though it was also the time I firmly decided to leave and that was, in part, due to the storylines. I truly believe that the show started to lose its way around this point with the Mario, Lewis and Grace love triangle, the Frank, Charlie and Ferne love triangle, the Diags, Tom and Fran storyline, Lockie and Danni – it was all too much and, more importantly, I am not sure the viewers cared.

But back when I had just come out of the house I was still so weak and not really on top of things so I gave it little thought – it was enough to just focus on getting through each day to be honest and I was trying desperately to keep up with all the get-well messages. I knew there were some messages from Joey I needed time to reply to properly. It was important to get the wording right and I couldn't rush it. I hadn't been ignoring him deliberately; it was just exhaustion. But it turns out that when he didn't hear from me he panicked and the Essex grapevine went into overdrive. He called Arg, who in typical Arg fashion dramatically told him I looked awful. It must have been this that prompted Joey to call me. I missed the first one but then he tried again and I was so happy to hear from him! I told him that the doctors thought I had Crohn's disease and he was just amazing, so upbeat. He kept telling me that I would be okay, that he knew I would be safe and fine, that I was such a strong girl. We ended the call as I was out and about, but I felt on a high for the rest of the day. Later that night we spoke again, this time for over three hours and we discussed absolutely everything. It just felt so good to be speaking to him, and that's the problem with us: this chemistry overrides everything – especially common sense which tells us we just shouldn't be together. It isn't healthy, as we have discovered after lots of heartache.

We arranged to meet up properly and it ended up falling on Valentine's Day, which was lovely, but not deliberate, and then we just slipped back into our old routine like we always do. It was so lovely to cuddle on the sofa and snuggle up. Everything just went back to the way it always does with us and we started to spend all our time together. That's what it always comes down to, when we get together we never need or want anyone else, we just exist in this Sam/Joey bubble of intensity and all the reasons that we broke up just disappear. But there is a real problem with Essex and the show really, that everyone is determined to put a label on everything and a timeline until there is a boyfriend/girlfriend title, before you move in together, get married and have a baby. I see it even with Billie and Greg now. Nelly isn't even one year old and the first question Billie is asked is when she wants to have the next one! I know that in the past she said she would like two babies close together so they grow up like me and her did, but, seriously, in her first post-baby shoot they were asking her and Greg when they would be trying again and when the big day was. Billie hadn't even had her stitches out! It is a function of living your life in the public eye – I know that and I know it goes with the territory, but sometimes it can harm things, especially with me and Joey as he gets easily spooked, and having all the papers and magazines pushing us down the aisle wasn't going to help us to recover some balance and normality in our relationship.

We took things slowly and tried to keep it quiet and not label it. I also knew that if we were going to give it a go, then certain things had to be different right from the start – I needed to confide less in friends so that our business stayed between us and us alone. I needed to drink less to cut down the chance of rows (though this wasn't a problem as I had virtually cut it out of my diet now to help with the flare-ups). We talked about it all and he maintained that it wasn't so much that he wanted to change me and stop me having fun, it was that he couldn't handle me when I was drunk as it gave him all sorts of paranoia. I pointed out that it wasn't that he didn't like what I did when I was drunk, it was that he didn't like his own thoughts when I was drunk – they were two very different things and I couldn't be held accountable for his demons. It was important to me that he knew this and accepted it before we tried to move forward. That said, it was less of an issue as mad all-nighters of partying were long gone as far as I was concerned. He knew he needed to change too – he was jealous and moody and could be very selfish, very his-way-or-the-highway – and I needed compromise from him too. The main thing I needed from him was his time – he had to make more time for us and manage his work diary properly so that we had a life like a normal couple – seeing each other one night a month is not normal and we had let it become so. We needed to re-group and put us first if we stood any chance of making it.

Crohn's and how to spot it

- Crohn's disease is an inflammatory bowel condition which affects 115,000 people in the UK. Inflammation is the body's reaction to injury or irritation, and can cause redness, swelling and pain.

- Crohn's is sometimes described as a chronic condition. This means that it is on-going and life-long, although you may have periods of good health (remission) as well as times when symptoms are more active (relapses or flare-ups).

- There is no cure for Crohn's but drugs and sometimes surgery can give long periods of relief from symptoms.

- No one knows for sure what causes it but it could be a combination of factors, including the genes a person has inherited, an abnormal reaction of the immune system to certain bacteria in the intestines and is probably triggered by something in the environment like viruses, bacteria or stress.

- Its symptoms include: pain, diarrhoea, vomiting, weight loss and fatigue.

- If you have any questions you should contact: www.crohnsandcolitis.org.uk or call 0845 130 2233.

11

Bigger and Better

My Style Makeover

The resignation chat did not go very well and they were desperate to accommodate me in any way they could if I would stay. It was a hard decision but inevitable given all I'd been through. It had been building. Scenes like the one with Mum and Billie, where we discussed the impact of my diagnosis and got very upset, were hard to film. It took a while to get it right as it was so upsetting for them both, especially Mum, and I tried really hard to hold it together, I didn't want to cry on screen. But as I sat there it just didn't feel right putting her through this for the sake of TV. It was weird when that episode aired. Me and Joey were sat next to each other on my sofa, cuddling up, and he was telling me it would be okay, and nobody had any idea that we were even back together at that point. I liked that we had something just for us but I also knew we needed to protect it now we didn't have any storyline pressure. We kept it quiet – I really do believe you can keep things out of the papers if you want to – and all was well until one night we were snuggled in bed and Joey put a photo of us on Instagram. He argued it was okay as you couldn't see our faces, but it was obvious it was us. He deleted it immediately, but the damage was done. It had been seen and now everyone was talking about our reconciliation – just the pressure we wanted to avoid and right around the time he was doing press for his new show, which I hoped was a coincidence . . .

The day after the picture 'outing' us, Joey had a morning of PR which started with *Heat* magazine and obviously the first question they asked Joey was who was in the picture. They pushed and pushed for him to say my name and he tried to be diplomatic and say that he was touched by how much everyone wanted us back together and even used our magazine nickname of 'Jam' to try to humour them off the scent. It didn't work, but it still wasn't official until a few days later when we were followed and papped due to what could only have been a tip-off, which really pissed me off given how hard we had worked to carve out some space to get things back on track before the fans, and the show, found out. Again, it seemed weird to me that all of a sudden, the press were on to us.

We were out in Brentwood for Greg's birthday. I had invited Joey, but for a bit later on. He had had meetings with his manager and Lime. Bizarrely, given he wanted to keep his new projects close to his chest, they decided to have that highly confidential meeting in Tarantino's, in the full public gaze where anyone could overhear, interrupt for autographs or just generally break it up. There were pap pictures of him having his meeting and then being greeted by Gemma, Bobby, Gemma's mum and Jess Wright, who all sat down for a chat and a catch-up. Of course, as soon as people saw him with the cast and the Lime producers, the story was that he was going back into *TOWIE*, just as it had been announced I was leaving – helpful! We waited for Joey to arrive and I ordered for him.

He arrived at the restaurant, Alec's, and sat down, and it was weird as it was the first time he had been back with the family since we had got back together and we were both really nervous about how it would go. My family have always been great and never interfered in my romantic life. When me and Joey rowed non-stop, when the Dubai slap story broke, when we got engaged, even though people didn't think we were ready for such a big commitment, Mum and Billie never said a word for or against or in any way tried to change my mind or influence me. They were deliberately the opposite of Joey's family in that way. My mum always said that she never doubted how much we loved each other, despite all the other crap that went on. But this time was different. They had seen me going to pieces over the jungle – properly have a break-down – and then the *Celebrity Big Brother* house and the illness.

My mum has always been, and always will be, convinced that my Crohn's flare-up was all to do with the stress and misery of Joey being in the jungle and the break-up. She says it is obvious that I punished my poor body. Everything shut down in self-preservation mode and then I went into the house, being cut off from everything with no phone, no Twitter, no family or friends, and my body said 'enough' – and that was that. Mum says, in fact they all say, they had been so scared of the Sam when Joey was in the jungle as I was so far away from my normal self, whereas day to day I was so easy-going and chilled. I was partying, working out, starving myself – anything to make me forget my pain over Joey. It was like nothing mattered. So, whilst my mum was delighted to see me smiling again, she was protective of me and no one was going to hurt me or set me back, especially not Joey.

Anyway, Joey arrived and hugged and said hi to everyone and sat down before we became aware of a photographer in the bushes outside the window – clearly the photographer who had spotted Joey in Tarantino's had followed him here and was now snapping away at all of us at the table having a drink. Unless of course he had been tipped off. I was so angry as this was not what we had planned at all. Joey swore he would have known if he had been followed and I knew there was no way anyone would know we were here – Alec's is outside Brentwood and fairly tucked away – unless they had been tipped off. Joey seemed more bothered about the bizarre ponytail he was wearing and the fact his hair wasn't 'perfect', so he went outside to have a word with the guy and ask him not to use the photos. Instead, if the pap destroyed these shots, he promised we would give him a picture together a few days later.

We thought that was the end of it and we could get on with the evening ahead. I had just wanted a bit of time for us to get used to being a couple again without the pressure of everyone having an opinion on our business. That's when, in the past, everything had swiftly gone downhill, when everyone around us starts having an opinion and butting in with well-meaning 'advice'. In the end all that bartering with the pap made no difference as he sold the pictures on anyway, to *Heat* magazine as it turned out, and they ran them as a front-page story with the headline: 'Joey and Sam finally go public – friends tell *Heat* that "their attraction is magnetic"'.

Joey was doing lots of press for his show, so of course our relationship came up. It was bound to after the front page of *Heat*, so although we didn't discuss it beforehand, he gave them the low-down on where we were with things. He told the *Sun on Sunday*: 'Obviously me and Sam do have feelings for each other. I have been seeing her again.' He told them that we saw each other after my diagnosis and that it went from there. 'I haven't had a serious girlfriend other than her. We'll always be close. She's a strong girl, Sam.'

He went on to use the interview to set the record straight on Amy: 'There was never a relationship between me and her. Ever. Maybe she thought it was a relationship but it weren't. It was just a laugh. There was never a romance ... she sets up quite a lot of pap shots herself, doesn't she? That's my life, innit? I always get followed by cameras.'

The whole Amy thing hadn't ended well really – she seemed confused about what her story was and then, perhaps when she felt it slipping away, she tried to get it back on track by messaging him a lot. He changed his number to stop her hounding him and then she slipped away from the headlines as quickly as she had arrived.

After the press, the pressure was immediate – it is like the public knowing and wanting us to have a 'happy ever after' is too much stress for us both, so we have to pull away and find fault and we did just that. The rows started up just a few weeks later and we fell into that old pattern of up and down, off and on. We had some fun times but the same old issues were still there, and the truth is that the old and complicated and paranoid Joey had started to surface and we slipped back into bad habits with each other. To be honest, we became impossible to handle. He still didn't seem to understand that you needed to dedicate time and effort to building a relationship and that meant time together. I was always so far down the pecking order, after his mates, his clubbing, his work and his shopping, he just didn't make me feel special. He didn't call me, make time for me, take me out or surprise me. He rarely bought me gifts, although when he did he was generous. I got bags and various other things over the years, including the watch he bought me for our last Christmas together, which he then withheld because of our row, and a pair of diamond earrings to thank me for planning the whole Fusey launch. I have my own money and have never been financially dependent on anyone and I can buy my own stuff, but now and again a little gift out of the blue is so romantic.

We limped on for a few months, deep down I knew that things were bad but I couldn't bring myself to deal with it. In the moments when I was honest with myself about how I felt, I realized I didn't even like him any more. I loved him but I didn't recognize the person he had become or I had fallen in love with. Suddenly, it was the summer and Nelly had just been born. Joey had been away for four weeks filming in Africa, contact was sporadic and we did the best we could but, when he got back, I hoped we'd have a good chunk of time together. It felt like a time to spend with family and loved ones – Billie was feeling good after the birth (I think she was high on all the hormones!) so she arranged a big afternoon out in London. I told Joey about it and he was up for it – this was our chance to be a normal couple and spend time with my new-born niece. Billie decided we were going to the Berkeley Hotel to have a posh afternoon tea and celebrate the birth of our beautiful Nelly, and of course I wanted my boyfriend by my side. It was so exciting, we all got dressed up – Billie had a gorgeous outfit for Nelly and she was in her amazing Silver Cross pram – it was such a proud moment walking down the street with our whole family showing off our new addition.

Joey and me had spoken the morning of the trip and I told him the plans and timings, he had said he was looking forward to it and would be there, but he wasn't. We all got there and waited for him; it got later and later and I was so embarrassed. In the end I had to confess to everyone that he wasn't coming. I was so angry and upset – it wasn't about us for once – this day had been about Nelly. I put on a brave face and made sure that Billie had a great time, but I was heartbroken he could treat me like this.

Whilst we were at the Berkeley, Joey rang in a fluster. I managed to get out of him that his manager had been called by a magazine who had come to them with a story saying that Joey had been cheating on me with a girl from up north. I kept asking him how they could be printing such a story, you need serious proof to make allegations like this, but he kept shouting and as usual was turning it around on me. In his eyes this was my fault. In one of the lowest blows ever he then accused me of planting this story and tried to blame me! Why on earth would I want anyone to think that my boyfriend would be cheating on me, let alone try to promote it. This was madness and a step too far, it was Billie's special day and he inflicted this on me.

I waited until we got back to Essex and sent him a long message telling him how I felt, but, as usual, he managed to twist things in his own mind so that, somehow, he was the injured party. If delusion was an Olympic sport, Joey would have a gold medal.

In the September we went away to Marbella with my family to formally celebrate Billie and Greg's engagement and the bickering and sniping got out of control, as it can sometimes when you feel hemmed in. It was always over the small things but they build and build. But for us nothing is private – we have an argument and before we can even sit down and talk it through the papers are running stories that we have split up again and then in everyone wades with their say and their take on things. This time they were right. The rows started before we even got there as Joey turned up at the airport, for a family holiday, with his sidekick, Danny Walia, in tow. It couldn't have been more inappropriate and yet Joey refused to travel without him. All of Greg's family were there – his mum, his sisters and their partners – and

Danny was staying in an apartment nearby so him and Joey could 'hang out'. It was all about celebrating Billie and Greg and yet he had already caused an atmosphere. Things just went from bad to worse and that was when I discovered the messages from girls.

On one of the days we were getting on, I was using his iPad to shop online as we relaxed. His Twitter and Instagram accounts were open and I couldn't resist taking a look. When I think back it makes me realize how destructive the whole relationship was – I am not – and never have been – that paranoid girl who scrolls down her boyfriend's phone to check up on him. And yet there I was doing just that, looking through his inbox to see that he was following and messaging all sorts of random girls who were following and messaging him back. 'What's up, where have you been?', 'Been thinking about you', 'You going out this weekend?' etc. There was also loads of WhatsApp activity. Don't get me wrong, there was nothing explosive there and, to the best of my knowledge, it was just banter and he never cheated on me, but it still hurt and it was still inappropriate. Most of all, it got me thinking about what on earth I was doing with someone I didn't trust, who had such double standards and who was being so disrespectful. What grated the most was the fact that he had gone mental just the week before and made me unfollow loads of people online, some were friends I'd had since school, just because he didn't like them seeing what I was doing.

'Why do you need to follow them?' he would ask of any men in my timeline or harmless people I'd met at PAs like

Scotty T (Scott Timlin from *Geordie Shore*). So I unfollowed them for a quiet life and yet here I was, looking at all his 'harmless banter'. Apparently he couldn't unfollow these girls as it would be 'rude.'

Of course we had a massive row and Joey left our villa and went to stay with his sidekick, Danny. In fact, in the short time we were there he packed his bags twice and left me to go and stay at Danny's – yet again making it all about him and casting a shadow over what was such a happy time for Billie and Greg. The thing about Joey is that he is so black and white, unless he is the one in the wrong, and then he is always right. It got so bad that one night when we were all out at the casino, he went mental when I went to the bar and ordered a gin and tonic. He just couldn't see how irrational he was being about me when he was the one following and messaging models who clearly fancied him. It was like he knew things between us weren't going to last and he was trying to line up my replacement in advance.

The night before we were due to fly home was the worst row of all. He stomped off to Danny's villa again and I decided I didn't want to go anywhere near him, so I told him to fly home on his own and I would stay on with my family. I assumed he would tell the press, if they asked, that he was always due to fly home before me as he had to start filming and I was staying on with the family to spend some time with my grandparents. To be honest, at that point, I really didn't care what he said. I was utterly exhausted, in fact I feel weepy and drained even having to think about it for this book. It brings it all back and it was such a dark time. In all honesty I remember feeling glad to see the back of him. I was in a permanent state of anxiety, desperate to keep the peace so that we didn't ruin things for Billie. I was also embarrassed, I wanted people to think we were grown up and really trying to make things work this time, but all they saw were petty rows and Joey's dark moods that left everyone walking around on eggshells. It was horrendous and we parted furious with each other. I was determined not to think about it or let him ruin the last bit of the holiday, he was officially off-limits and the family knew not to bring him up. I just wanted us to have fun. I decided we would deal with it when I got back to the UK. That was until the following morning when I opened the *Sun* and saw I'd been 'dumped'.

According to a 'source', he dumped me 'for a second time following a string of rows'. The paper reliably informed me and the rest of its readers that we had been going through a rough patch 'for a while' but that it got too much for Joey whilst we were away: 'They are constantly bickering and falling out. It's not been pretty. The atmosphere between them wasn't healthy and Joey simply had enough – he just had to get away.'

So there it was, the 'truth' about my relationship on the front of a tabloid newspaper when I was in Spain with my friends and family and hadn't spoken to a soul about what had gone on. And there Joey and his agent Dave were, back in the UK, to my mind, looking for publicity. I called him right away and accused him outright of letting Dave plant the story to stoke things up and get back at me – it is exactly the sort of petty thing Joey would do. Of course he denied it, but we both knew the truth. There were only two of us who knew how bad things were, and one of us had flown straight back to our manager. And it certainly hadn't been me.

It was all falling apart and taking on its own momentum, but the headline in the *Sun* was a defining moment for me. I was so angry when I got back that we didn't really talk. We didn't make any time to fully discuss what had happened and we only saw each other about three or four times after I got back from Spain and then had the Doddle (the parcel delivery service) photo shoot straight away. Even before the row in Spain, on average we were only seeing each other once a week if we were lucky and it just isn't enough if you want a solid relationship. We both know how to push each other's buttons and always have and I used to tell him that we were better off just forgiving, forgetting and moving on. But Joey has always been one to over-analyse everything and read more into it than needed to be done and grudges would form and they would last. He could be manipulative to the point where I just didn't know where I was. I was certain he was behind that headline and to me, planting a story on your own girlfriend, well, that was a new low.

But I also had other things on my mind and that involved moving forward with my career now that *TOWIE* was over. I've been open about the fact that it was so emotional to say goodbye to *TOWIE* in the first place, but the way my final episode was handled as I said earlier, gutted me if I am honest. I think back to some of the goodbyes that I was involved in – Mark Wright, Lydia, even Lucy Meck, whose big Christmas exit was just one series before mine – and I didn't even get more than two minutes' airtime. I felt really sad and betrayed after so long on the show and it affected me quite badly, as knocks like that can. Adam called the producers to ask why it had been cut right down and to let them know how sad I felt. They came up with some random new rule (that they had kept to themselves) that nobody, no matter how long they had been in the show, got a filmed send-off any more. Apparently this new rule meant that it left the door open for the star to return if things didn't work out. I'm not sure how not saying goodbye to me after twelve series left the door open any wider than if they had allowed me a few minutes to say what I wanted to and leave with all loose ends tied up, but there you are. I felt like they were so angry at me leaving that they punished me the only way they knew how. But actually behaviour like that undervalues what you have given to something you have worked hard on for a long time. It makes it easier to leave and switch off and move on – and that's just what Adam helped me to do with so many exciting things I could only ever have dreamed about whilst still in the show.

The first thing to launch was my fragrance. I was so very excited; I genuinely love it. The scent is a vanilla top note – my absolute favourite – mixed with iris and benzoin heart notes and a blend of musk laced with caramel in the base notes. I know lots of people think that stars from reality TV shows are lazy and without talent, that they 'luck out' and don't put work in, but that isn't true at all in my case. The team from Per Scent came to me with the proposition that I create a fragrance that girls would love and it was a dream come true! I am such a girlie girl and I have so many perfumes it is ridiculous. Most of them are lined up on my dressing table like beautiful objects. I had a vision right from the word go as it is so my area of expertise. I knew how I wanted the bottle to look, the colour of the fragrance, the packaging, the lettering, even the stopper. I have always loved to smell nice. I worked bloody hard on every aspect of my fragrance and I couldn't be prouder of myself or the development team I worked with. They are so talented and they helped me so much with the whole process – they let me lead at the same time as being there to help and advise when I needed it. Just putting my name to something, whatever it is, is not the direction I want to be going in. I want to be known for my integrity and having my head screwed on and being a good businesswoman who understands her market – whether it is books, fragrances, DVDs, lashes or Minnies. I'm there and a hundred per cent involved or I won't be referenced.

It feels like an amazing thing to have learned so many new skills that I never would have otherwise. I am a nightmare to buy for when it comes to scent – just ask anyone who knows me: I am the fussiest! So it took me a long time to get the smell and the packaging spot on – over eighteen months and the whole thing began when I was in the thick of rebranding Minnies with Mum, Libby and Billie, and still filming full time for the show. I kept it really quiet in those early stages so that I could work on it behind the scenes and learn as much as I could. There was no way I wanted to put out any old crap! For me the big thing is that the scent lasts on the skin for as long as possible, so that meant that the alcohol content was higher, but the balance had to be right so it wasn't overpowering and gave you a headache. I really think it fits my target market brilliantly – it is smart, sassy, sophisticated and the bottle and packaging is so classy. Billie and Mum are obviously biased but they do genuinely love it and wear it, even Nelly can recognize it when I wear it to give her a cuddle – it makes her smile! Mum and Billie and Libby were a great help and support when I was trying to find the right feel and smell for the fragrance.

I couldn't have been prouder to see my debut scent go straight to number one – it took just three weeks and it beat scents from Britney Spears and One Direction to be crowned the number-one celebrity fragrance launch of 2014. I was told that 'record numbers' flew off the shelves, placing it in the top three biggest-selling scents across all ranges. I literally didn't stop smiling. My thing was always beautiful packaging, obviously a great smell, but, above all, affordability. I also overtook Alesha Dixon's Rose Quartz, which went into second place, whilst One Direction's That Moment and Britney Spears's Fantasy took third and fourth respectively. It sounds trite and like it is an obvious thing to say, but I am of the generation for celebrity perfume, don't forget, and I used to be gutted when my idols brought out a perfume that I couldn't afford – I really never did see the point, especially when your demographic was so young and they were saving up pennies to buy your latest product. You have to be accessible or what is the point? You can never forget or exclude your core market and I was determined not to do that to mine. I have always been open about the fact that I look up to Victoria Beckham and Elizabeth Hurley as business brands – and it isn't because their stuff is high-end luxury goods that you need a lot of money for. It is because they are two women who know their market inside out, who strive and give it a hundred per cent at all times, who travel to promote their brand despite having kids, who design, who sign it all off, who oversee every little detail. That means that their brand is essentially them through and through. Their products are confident because they are genuine and that was all I wanted for my fragrance – for the people who bought it to know I had worked hard on it and that I wore it every day as it was something I loved.

Perfect party look

- Watch the blusher – there is nothing worse than those cheeks that look like rosy apples when you are going for the sexy and sophisticated look.

- Make sure eye make-up is blended in – use an eyeshadow brush, it helps to get right into the corner so that the whole eyelid is covered.

- To avoid the awful foundation watermark line, smooth the liquid down past your jaw and to the top of your neck, it helps to even it out.

- I know I would say this, but my fake eyelashes really are the best! I love the fact that there's a set for every occasion. They all make you feel like a million dollars, but the night-time ones are so glam they make me feel like a film star. I love a dramatic and sultry look for the evening, lots of lash and mascara is a great combo if you're out to impress.

- I never go anywhere without my lip gloss and hairbrush, both are great for a quick 'touch-up' when you are on the go.

- For the 'beauty look', I use loads of different brands and am always keen to try something new that's on the market – you should shop around and change your products every now and then so that your skin has a change. I mix designer and high street brands so I love Naked and Sleek, but I also use a great Laura Mercier foundation. I have fun experimenting with eyeshade, though Billie is the queen of eye make-up and makes me look like an amateur! I hope Nelly inherits her skills and not mine!

- Use lip liner to perfect your pout. Me and Billie love our make-up and used to spend hours applying and removing our lipstick, kissing our mirror and imagining it was our Prince Charming – Mark from Westlife for Billie and Mickey Mouse for me. It always makes me smile when I think of us doing that and imagine Nelly doing it with her mates – how cute will that be!

- Never go to bed with your make-up on, it is a total sin and makes your skin very unhappy.

- I try to keep my hair colour natural these days. I love it. Now that I have left the show I'm enjoying a new pared-down look. Maybe it is just what happens when you get older but I've definitely grown in confidence. I am up for trying new things, new looks, and it feels great to have that freedom at last to feel good about making my own choices.

- Recently there have been false claims that I've had work done on my face. I was trying a new statement look at London Fashion Week and had help from a new make-up artist, and now apparently I've had fillers and and eye lift! These claims are really hurtful and I don't want to send the wrong message to my fans. I'm twenty-four now, not eighteen, so of course my face has changed!

12

Billie, the Baby and the Future

From the minute that Billie announced her pregnancy, we were all giddy with excitement in a way that I can't explain – we all went a bit mad. Mum kept calling Billie's baby 'my baby!' If Prince George was the nation's baby then Nelly was most definitely Essex's!

Nelly was unplanned really, in the sense that Billie and Greg weren't actively trying to get pregnant. She and Greg were only young. They were working hard to build their life together and having some fun along the way; a baby wasn't really on the immediate agenda. She had thought something was up, as she hadn't been feeling herself and she had missed her period, which never happened to Billie. I think she knew deep down, but she was too scared to do the test and find out for sure. It is the loveliest bombshell really.

Greg knew that she was pregnant before she did it turns out. He said she looked different and all these spots were erupting on her face, which isn't very Billie either as she has the best skin in the family! Greg says that buying the test was a comedy moment of its own as she sent him to the chemist to get it in case anyone spotted her – can you imagine the headlines if she had been papped and it was a false alarm, or worse, that they thought she was buying it for me! They were both in shock really – they had been together for a couple of years, had a lovely home and a nice thing going on, and Billie and I have grown up around babies so we weren't under any illusions about what hard work they could be and how your life is never the same again. It was definitely a life-changing moment to know she was going to be responsible for ever for a tiny little person.

Amazingly Billie managed to keep it quiet for two whole weeks from me and Mum. That in itself is miraculous enough as we can't keep any kind of secret in my family! I hadn't really noticed anything different in her as it was so hectic with the build-up to Christmas, my birthday, New Year, etc., and I was so preoccupied with worrying about going into *CBB*, that I didn't really notice any difference in her behaviour. At that point I was still in my manic and slightly self-obsessed phase where I was dieting and working out like a demon, worrying about making sure that I looked good on camera, so that took up a lot of my headspace.

Anyway, she invited me and Mum round for dinner, which was very normal as Billie is a great hostess and loves cooking and entertaining. She is so good at it and everything is always perfect – the food, the table, everything is like it is out of a magazine shoot! We went round and she cooked a lovely meal and she was gearing up to tell us both, but after dinner we all got cosy in the lounge and snuggled down and, before I knew it, I was fast asleep on her sofa, so that plan went out of the window! Anyway, a few days later she finally announced it and, apart from the day that Nelly was born, I have never been happier. Me and Mum cried and were just so happy for them and I could see how relieved she and Greg were that we were so excited for them. I don't think I have ever been more delighted, mainly as we had talked about this moment since we were really young – we used to play mummies and babies and house all the time and talk about when we would be grown-ups and have our own. We had dollies and prams and names for them all and now here we were. Billie kept the news fairly low-key and found Christmas hard – she was so tired, which was difficult for her as she is usually the one with bags of energy, but she pushed on through and Mum was brilliant at looking after her. She was so chuffed at becoming a young nan (that had always been part of the plan, apparently!) and she was on hand from day one.

It turns out that the baby wasn't the only surprise for the family. Greg had a big plan up his sleeve – he whisked Billie away to the Maldives for a New Year break and got down on one knee to propose! He had it all down to the final detail and had spoken to Mum and Dad beforehand and the ring is exquisite – so perfectly Billie in every way. Greg and I are known as the planners in the family – we are always organizing nights out, holidays away, gatherings, etc., and we love a list and a plan – but this was on another level! He organized it perfectly.

Billie loves to tell the story of the proposal, she gets all soppy when she talks about it and says that it couldn't have been any more romantic or emotional as he got down on one knee and told her he wanted to spend the rest of his life with her. He said: 'I love you. I want to spend the rest of my life with you and I know our baby will be just as beautiful as you are. Will you marry me?'

He cried a lot too, which set Billie off – that's one of the things I love most about Greg, he is so comfortable in his own skin that he doesn't mind showing his emotions. They looked so happy when they came back. I was bursting for them both – it felt like such a new start for us all and, weirdly, got me through my time in the house and my illness, knowing that Billie was growing a new little life inside her that I would meet in the summer.

Nelly made her debut on *TOWIE* fairly early on, when Billie filmed one of her antenatal appointments, the one where she went for the scan and found out the sex. There was then a brilliant *TOWIE* baby celebration party at Nu Bar where Billie and Greg cut into a cake with the words, 'He or She? Open and See'. They cut into it and picked up a slice of cake to reveal pink icing and everyone went mad! I think the *TOWIE* girls were giddy anyway as Billie is the first of the group to have a baby but, somehow, the fact it was going to be a little girl they could buy loads of dresses and shoes for made them all the more excited. I think they thought she was going to be like their own real-life dolly! I know it made a few extra broody and since she has been born there have been long queues for cuddles – even Arg has got involved! It was a great episode and it will be so special to show Nelly one day that she was the star of the show even in Mummy's tummy.

Billie took to pregnancy like a natural and managed to look amazing all the way through. I know it is a cliché but she glowed from the inside out. Her skin, nails and hair all looked amazing and she had a fairly easy time of it. Fashion-wise, she looked a million dollars. She chose some bold colours and styles to show off her very neat bump. She hardly put on any weight until the end – only two stone in total, but she ate well and really looked after herself. Mum warned her that a lot of women see their first pregnancy as an excuse to pig out – and let's face it, we are all on diets most of the time or denying ourselves something in order to stay slim, so I can more than understand why some really go for it. But as Mum said, it doesn't just magically disappear with the baby when it comes out! Billie and I talked about how tempting it must be to really go for it (unless you are Victoria Beckham, who never looks like she puts on even an ounce!), but Billie was good and just kept telling herself what went on would have to come off when the baby was out. She wanted most of all to be healthy and grow the baby well; everything else came second.

She got photographed wearing some really good maternity bits and it got us thinking about a range in the future, but one of us would have to be pregnant – or maybe both at the same time! Can you imagine? My mum would go into nanny over-drive! Anyway, the pregnancy went smoothly, apart from one scary moment when she fainted at Harry's birthday party at

Balans in Soho. I wanted to get her to A&E to get checked over but she wouldn't hear of it – she just wanted to go home to her bed and sleep, and she was fine after that. She was just overdoing it a bit as she worked throughout the pregnancy with filming, the shop and developing Jam Kidswear. Neither one of us is very good at putting our feet up or being 'ill' – we are like our mum and just get on with it – but looking back she probably needed to take it a bit easier.

So the pregnancy rolled on and suddenly we were nearing the due date. Billie had been to see a medium about the pregnancy and baby a few weeks before and he had said that the birth was imminent, which threw us a bit, as we had booked a night at Pennyhill Park Spa for some nice relaxing treatments before the baby arrived. We spent ages worrying if we should cancel – we certainly didn't want to be far from home if something happened. But I wanted to spoil Billie with a pregnancy massage and facial, and for her to feel good about herself before labour started. In the end we chanced it and thank God we did as Nelly ended up being overdue! We would have missed out on all that pampering, which was lovely and meant that Billie felt all fresh for the labour – not that she felt fresh afterwards!

We had already agreed that me and Mum would be Billie's birthing partners. She had asked us as soon as she announced she was pregnant, so we knew that, when the time came, we would both be in the room with Greg. I'd had experience of being a birthing partner before as I'd been a partner for one of my best friends Jerri when she had her two babies. I knew the thing was to remain calm and offer lots of massage to help with the pain and the contractions.

The day of the birth finally arrived. Billie came round to my house early in the morning to say she thought labour was starting as she was feeling weird, that she wasn't in pain and that there weren't any contractions, but that things were starting to happen. I was due to work that day in London – I had a Radio 1 show with my friend the DJ Sarah-Jane Crawford – and I immediately told Billie I would cancel and be there for her. She insisted I go – she said it could take hours for anything to actually happen and there was no point in gathering everyone at her house just to sit around with her, so I went and did the show.

When I came out and turned on my phone, Mum called immediately to say that Billie's contractions had started, so I jumped in the car and headed back to Essex and my house to change. I was caked in make-up from the job (it is so annoying to have to wear make-up all the time, even on the radio, but the alternative is to be papped without it and that would NOT be a good look!) and had so much product and hairspray on my styled hair – can you imagine if I'd turned up at the hospital looking like I was off to a photo shoot! I was like a woman possessed as I scrabbled around for a tracksuit to put on, took off my make-up, tied my hair back and jumped in my car again.

I live on quite a narrow country lane and am usually very careful about driving down there sensibly as cars can come flying round the corner, but that day I was the one driving like a bat out of hell! I flew round the corner and there was a van right in front of me, and I sort of pushed him off the lane and clipped his wing mirror. Normally I am such a careful and polite driver – I actually hate bad driving in others – but that day I just thought to myself, *I'm not stopping. I have got to get there now and not miss a minute.* So I carried on driving! I know it was bad and I would like to take this opportunity to apologize to that driver: if you are reading, it was an emergency, honest! He looked right into my car and definitely recognized me. I thought to myself there would probably be a headline in the paper the next day. That would be just my luck! But none of that mattered, just getting to Billie's side was my sole focus.

I tried to calm down before I went into the room as I didn't want to disturb the vibe and when I entered Billie was on the gas and air and the room was very peaceful. My mum and Greg were sitting with her and chatting, but it was very early stages, so I sat down and the wait began. The day went on and things progressed slowly and the pain kept going up a notch, but Billie was very calm and controlled. There was no shouting or screaming, more low moaning: she was really getting into the zone. But the day dragged on and she got tired and started asking for an epidural, which she had been adamant that she didn't want. It was crystal clear on the birthing plan in big letters, and she had told us all that, despite what she said if she was in pain, we were to remind her of the fact that she really didn't want it and to keep her away from it at all costs – easier said than done when a woman is in the thick of labour and demanding one! She had been really worried that it might affect the baby and make it really drowsy. Billie didn't end up having an epidural, just gas and air.

Eventually she got into the birthing pool to help with the pain and Greg went off to get some supplies for us – I felt bad for Billie but she was in her own world of pain and I was starving! Off Greg went to M&S and came back with bags of food. He sat in the chair and got stuck in to a sandwich and crisps as me and Mum sat on the floor next to Billie. What happened next was one of the most comedy moments of the whole labour. Greg was eating a packet of beef-flavoured Hula Hoops, crunching away in the corner, whilst Billie was having another contraction. He came over to pat her on the shoulder and let her know he was right there, with the words: 'How are you, babe? You're doing great.'

Oh my God, she went MENTAL. I have never seen Billie like it! She turned round in the pool and screamed: 'Get away from me. You STINK. I don't even want you in here. You aren't doing anything to help anyway, get out!!!'

Poor Greg didn't know what to do and looked at my mum in shock. She was hilarious – she gave him a look that said, 'Just let it go over your head. Look at the situation she is in.'

So he slunk back over to his chair and kept his head down for twenty minutes, but before he tried again he went to wash his hands and find some chewing gum!

That was the one moment really when she lost it and it had to be poor Greg who got the brunt of it, but that's traditional in a way. Then I nearly had a row with one of the nurses who decided to come in and tell us that there were only two birthing partners allowed, though Billie had always said she wanted three and no one had ever said that was a problem. This woman didn't seem to want to listen and was adamant one of us had to leave. Obviously Billie needed my mum and Greg in there so I offered to wait outside. But Billie was having none of that and I saw the nurse get a flash of what Greg had just experienced, as Billie well and truly stood her ground and insisted I stay as I had done this twice before. In the end, the nurse changeover happened at just the right time, and the new one who came in was lovely and far less of a jobsworth! She let me stay as Billie was crying at the thought of us all not being there like she wanted.

There is one image I will always have in my head and it is of Greg on the chair trying to sleep with a funny sheet over his head and me on this birthing beanbag with a similar sheet wrapped all round me. We looked like a couple of ghosts – I am not sure Billie saw the funny side! But as the night drew in, we were exhausted and I just couldn't keep my eyes open. My mum was phenomenal – she didn't close her eyes once in thirty-six hours. I don't know how she did it. She just kept willing Billie on, talking to her and stroking her face and hair. It was an amazing thing just to see them together, to see how much Billie needed our mum and how lucky we were to have her there for us.

We all had roles as things started to quicken up. Mum was the cheerleader and instrumental in keeping Billie away from the epidural as we knew she would regret it later. As she got to eight centimetres dilated, she started insisting on having it, but we were all shouting and cheering her on, telling her: 'You've come so far without one, don't give in now.' I was on hand with the water spray and fan and was massaging her to help with the contractions. It was the middle of summer and Billie was so hot and sticky. She said the only thing that kept her sane was the water spray and now she says she would urge any woman in labour to make sure they have some packed as it saved her sanity. Greg was dipping in and out; I felt a bit sorry for him with two women there who were all over it and seemed to know exactly what to do. And then the pushing started and that's when Billie really wanted him by her side. Billie had been adamant that Greg was NOT allowed down the business end. He was to stay firmly by her head at all times and me and Mum were to be down there telling her what was happening! She started pushing and, in all, it took an hour to push Nelly out and, my goodness, it was amazing. Billie did an incredible job. She didn't scream once. She barely raised her voice at all, but was totally in the zone of deep breathing and focussing. I would have been shouting the place down but I have never seen her so zen. She just got on with the job in hand and, actually, I think it must be much easier to get through it if you stay as calm as possible (easier said than done, I know!). She was amazing, like an Amazon. Out Nelly came and they put her straight on Billie's chest and I will remember for ever the look on Billie and Greg's faces. It hit me straight in the chest seeing them beaming – they kissed each other and they were both crying, and Billie just kept saying: 'I can't believe it. I can't believe she is here.'

It was the most precious moment and I am so privileged to have seen it – I have never seen Billie's face radiate such joy like that, ever. During the birth she had ripped a bit and I was still at the foot of the bed when the nurses started to try to sort her out and put some stitches in. The other priceless moment came when Billie whispered to me nervously, 'Is it all right down there? Does it look okay?' It made me laugh so much that she was asking me to confirm that it all looked normal down there after she had just pushed out a baby, and I reassured her it looked fine to me! What amazed me was that the minute Nelly was out Billie's stomach just shrunk right back down. It deflated like some kind of balloon. All in all it was a thirty-six-hour labour and it had been such an amazing thing to be a part of it. I went home and showered, got into bed and had the longest sleep of my life. I slept for hours, God knows how Billie felt if I was that knackered just from watching! She stayed in hospital for a bit to rest, but then wanted to return home where she was inundated with visitors from both sides of the family and, as soon as I woke up, I got straight back up there for more cuddles, and that set a pattern really – I am round there every day getting my fix.

So Billie went home and Mum moved in with her for a few weeks to help. Before the birth, they had sort of settled on Elsie – they loved all the old-fashioned names that were coming back – but as soon as she came out Billie said: 'She doesn't look like an Elsie.' I had to agree, she really didn't – with those eyes and those lashes and her face, Elsie just didn't suit her. So she was nameless for a week or so and then suddenly my mum had a revelation. She was sitting in bed with Billie going through the name book and cuddling the baby and she just said, 'She looks like a Nelly.' And that was it – everyone agreed she looked just like a little Nelly and the name suited her perfectly. Greg loved it so much, though she already had so many nicknames. Doodles is the family favourite but she also goes by the names of Nelly-Noo and Little Lady. It was a few days later, when I went round there with my mum for cuddles, that Billie broke the news her middle name would be Samantha. I was honestly so choked. I couldn't believe it – what an honour.

That was it really. Nelly just settled into our lives as if she had always been around and Billie took to it all brilliantly. She is the most wonderful mummy you could imagine. I can't remember what Billie was like without Nelly. She's brought so much joy to us all and Nelly is such a daddy's girl. It melts my heart when she sees Greg come in from work at night – her legs go like mad and she starts squealing and laughing – she is such a happy baby. And as for my mum, she's addicted! As soon as Billie was pregnant Mum started buying things – a cot, a changing table, etc. I said, 'Where is all that going to go in Billie's house? She's got stuff already.' Her reply was priceless: 'It isn't for Billie's, it's for mine. The baby will have two of everything – one for their house and one for mine.'

I am not sure if the arrival of Nelly made me think differently about my situation with Joey. But, timing-wise, it coincided with me focussing my mind on what I wanted – or perhaps more accurately – on what I wasn't getting from our relationship. I saw Billie starting such an exciting stage of her life – she was with the man she was going to marry and they were going to bring up a little baby. They had their unit sorted and that certainty Billie had about her life was so lovely to see, it made it even more obvious in a way that I was never going to have that with Joey. We may have had the chemistry but it felt a bit like immature drama in comparison to building a proper future with a life partner and raising a little person to be the best that they could be. It wasn't, as some press reports made out, that I was desperate to shove Joey down the aisle, it was that I knew we'd never get there and I was wasting my time trying to force it. I had a boyfriend who didn't even want to make time to see me, who preferred going out with his mates and getting drunk, who was messaging random girls from clubs for attention, who didn't show my family, or me, any respect and who cried all the time about situations he has created. Ever since we got back from Marbella, and even after I was sure in my mind that he and Dave had planted that story, it still felt like I was the only one trying to salvage things. He even started accusing my mum of being horrible to him, despite the fact that in his book he says she was always lovely to him. I guess this is a mark of how messed up his mind was at the time and what I was dealing with. I have thought long and hard about what switched in my mind around this time and there genuinely wasn't one big 'light bulb moment,' I just got to the point where I'd had enough.

In Marbella, his behaviour had been a disgrace and I was mortified by what my family had seen. I just decided that I had done all I could and that I was wasting my life trying to make something work that wasn't right. I picked up my phone whilst I had the courage – it felt very 'now or never' – to have the chat. But he didn't pick up, so I sat down and drafted a long text message basically saying that we were over, that I'd had enough and couldn't do it any more. I poured my heart out and was very clear I felt it was for the best for both of us and that it wasn't up for discussion. This was my decision and I was sticking to it. I sent it at 13.54 p.m. on Sunday 5 October and immediately knew I had to get away, so I emailed my friend Benny in LA so he would get my message as soon as he woke up. I was asking him if I could come and stay in his spare room. I needed to know he was free as I didn't want to be spending every day out there on my own and I knew he would look after me. Given that they are eight hours behind out there, I didn't get a reply from him until the afternoon – he was like, 'Get on the flight!' So the rest of the day was spent calling Mum and Billie, asking advice (they were both saying, 'Just do it! Get away and have fun!') and FaceTiming Benny about what to pack and what we were going to do when I arrived. I booked the flights – a last-minute Virgin plane. I couldn't believe how expensive it was, but it was worth every penny to get away from the UK as soon as possible. I wasn't running away, I just needed to breathe. I sorted the flight, packed my case and it got to 8 p.m. and I realized Joey hadn't replied. In a way that made it easier and I was glad, even though I did find myself sneaking the odd look at my lock screen to see if anything was there.

I had sort of expected him not to reply. I knew he liked to

play games but also my tone had been firm. I also told him I was going away, although I didn't tell him where. I wrote my break-up message out on a piece of paper first to make sure it was absolutely right and then I typed it up on my phone after I had made a few changes. I was so tired of trying to make our relationship something it wasn't, tired of begging him to spend time with me. I lost count of the number of messages I sent him suggesting that we go out on a date night, or just snuggle up with a film. He never seemed to want to spend any time together, it was all about clubs, his mates and whatever else seemed to make him happy – it certainly wasn't me.

Although I had that slightly anxious feeling in my tummy once I had hit 'send', I also felt really proud of myself, that I had been strong and addressed the situation head on and in a grown-up way, all the things I knew Joey was incapable of. After 8 p.m. the landline rang and I saw it was Joey's number but I didn't pick up. I then got a text at 21.47 p.m. saying:

> I called ur house and mobile. Give me a call when
> u can talk please.

I tried not to think about it, I got all my clothes out on the bed as I tried to pick what to take, I got everything ready and did what I always did before I went away, I packed my case and took it down by the front door, leaving it open for the last-minute things I would add in the morning. I put my passport on the dresser next to the front door and then I could sleep well knowing it was all ready – except I didn't sleep a wink. I had this bizarre feeling in the pit of my stomach that Joey would turn up at my house. I can't explain it, I was lying in bed knowing that I needed to be asleep as I had a long flight ahead the next day, but instead I was listening out for all the cars going past my remote country lane, expecting one to stop, and it to be Joey.

It got really late, around midnight, and I was wide awake when I heard a car pull on to the drive. I was on my own so it was a little scary but I had been expecting him. There was a slight pause and then continuous knocking at the door. Before I had gone to bed I locked the door as usual and put the chain on. I could hear him calling my name, he was shouting, 'Sam, Sam, Sam, Sam, Sam' – he wasn't even pausing for breath, he was agitated and I felt a bit nervous. Then I heard his key in the lock and it turned and, suddenly, my front door was open and he was still calling my name. He was pushing the door but he couldn't get in because of the chain. The door was definitely open enough for him to clearly see the suitcase. His shouting got more frantic. I just thought: 'Shit, what shall I do?'

In the end I went downstairs, mainly so that he didn't wake up my neighbours, the last thing I needed was them complaining or calling the police because of noise disturbance. Because I had been so stressed I had broken out in masses of spots, so before I got into bed that night, I had covered my face in thick white spot cream! So I answered the door with a white face in my crappy PJs that I reserved for being on my own, I couldn't have looked less attractive but I didn't give it a second thought as I ran downstairs to stop the noise.

I opened the door and let him in, we sat down in the lounge and everything was a bit awkward. We made some small talk and then, all of a sudden, he produced this letter he had written. He was saying all the right things – that ending it was for the best, I was right to say we weren't compatible, etc. It was typical Joey, I'd ended things with him but here he was now, with his letter, trying to claim it as a mutual decision, if not his decision – he was manipulative until the end. I know him so well and I know it would have been important for him to write that so that, in his own mind, he felt like he had finished with me. Knowing Joey, he probably took a picture of the letter to keep up his sleeve for when people asked what had happened. I half expected it to end up on the front page of a tabloid. Then he asked where I was going – I think he assumed I was going to my mum's or maybe Marbella – when I said LA he said, 'What do you mean you're going to LA? Why are you going there, all that way?

I made it clear that I wasn't running from him and, looking back, it was the best thing I ever did. If I'd stayed at home for the week, I know I would have buckled and gone back to him – there's always that moment where you lose your nerve and wobble. I'm glad I decided to get away from Essex. We had a little kiss and he joked about what was on my face, we were both a bit choked and sad, it was the end and that's always hard.

But where he had forced the door trying to get in, it was broken and now I couldn't open it from the inside to let him out. What ensued was this comedy routine of him trying to go home and being unable to get through my front door. So in the end I had to let him out of the back door into the garden and he had to leave via the back gate. I received a text when he got home saying:

> In bed now. Sorry it has to be this way. Is the best
> for both of us.

I felt calmer once he had gone and got some sleep. In the morning I felt quite okay about the whole thing, I had a meeting with Adam and then my taxi arrived and I was off to the airport. It was all fine, I checked in and had a tea and boarded the plane but all of a sudden I had a meltdown, where I cried for an hour solidly – the poor man next to me must have thought I was a complete loon! I had my scarf on and a zip-up jacket right over my chin and I curled up in my seat and just sobbed. I am not sure I was sad about the break-up, it was more the realization that I was on my own. This eleven-hour flight was the beginning of me being alone from now on. I couldn't help but play it all over in my head, wondering if I was doing the right thing. Everything haunted me, there was even a moment when I used the loo on the plane when I thought to myself: 'Amy and Joey had sex in a bathroom identical to this.' My mind was in meltdown.

Then I landed, Benny was there to meet me and that was it, I was in LA. I didn't meet any boys when I was there, I just wasn't interested. I had the best time as a single girl there doing loads of exciting and one-off things – I mean, meeting Kim Kardashian was the biggest highlight ever. But more than that, I just got back to being me, without the pressure of living my life being scared of someone else's mood swings. I realized how far I'd let myself drift away and I made a vow I would never allow that to happen again.

I was excited to be back when I landed in the UK, not least as I wanted to test out this new, strong me. It was great timing to hear that Joey was going away as soon as I landed, whether that was deliberate or not it was good news for me – it meant I could go out and not worry too much about bumping into him and his silly little mates. Then when he got home, I flew to Dubai with the family and Jess Wright, so there was no crossover time at all, which was such a blessing.

The final straw had been when I had been travelling back from Luisa Zissman's engagement party at her house and I got a phone call from a friend urging me to take a look at the Sunday *Mirror* website – apparently there was a video of Joey looking completely out of it that was getting loads of hits. I went straight on to take a look and, as I sat in the back of the cab, I felt so sad for him that it had come to this. I worried about him – where were his so-called mates when he needed them? Everyone knew what Joey was like when he lost control, he needed people around him to look out for him, see him home and make sure that things like this didn't happen. I don't know what came over me, but I called him. I had this strong need to know he was okay. He didn't pick up, but then I didn't really expect him to. I sent him a text, just saying that I was worried about him and hoped he was okay. The reply I got was astounding:

Don't worry about me, I will always be okay. Don't call me
again when you are drunk.

If I needed any reassurance I had done the right thing in
dumping him, here it was in black and white. I had called
him because I cared about him and he even managed to turn
that around into a dig about me going out and having a drink,
despite the fact that anyone could testify I wasn't even drunk.
I suppose that was the difference now, he was the one wan-
dering around LA without any real friends, out of control,
being filmed by strangers and then having the embarrassment of having those videos on the internet, and I was the
one who didn't need to care any more.

I didn't really have time to dwell on it as in November we
had an amazing holiday in Dubai with the girls, and that
included Nelly – she comes everywhere with us. Nelly is with
Billie, or one of the family, every single minute of the day. We
hired a yacht and danced, drank and partied away. Jess was
getting over the Ricky debacle and I was having the first real
downtime I'd managed since me and Joey had split. Mum
came and helped out with Nelly, and Carol and Mark Wright
senior came out too, which was lovely for Mum. The whole
trip was a blast – we really treated ourselves and were brilliantly well looked after. That's the thing about Dubai – it is so
easy to have a lovely holiday there. Everything you need is
right there on your resort doorstep, guaranteed sunshine and
sand – perfect for a girls' getaway. It was also really the first
time that I had felt body-confident in such a long time, since

well before my illness. All those months obsessing about my body and then being ill and looking skeletal and wishing I could put it back on – now I felt fresh, trim, toned and happy, at ease in a bikini. It was a real moment where I could see I was healthy and that all the exercise had really paid off.

The icing on the cake in terms of Joey was when he called me out there. We were floating out to sea on this amazing yacht, overlooking Dubai. The bubbles were flowing, it was boiling and my iPhone was plugged into the boat's music system down below deck. All of a sudden, the music stopped as the ringtone started. I ran down to see who it was and Joey's name flashed up. The crowd I was with all started urging me to answer it so I did. He was all a bit stuttery and awkward and would have heard the abroad ringtone. He said he was calling to apologize for being so rude to me when I called him in LA to see how he was. After he'd been so foul to me I blocked him on WhatsApp and deleted his number in case I ever felt sorry for him again. He obviously felt bad and would have been worried about the damage done to 'Brand Essex' but, as he had pointed out, he really wasn't my concern any more. It was a polite conversation and, knowing I was in Dubai with my family, he couldn't wait to get off the phone!

The fact that he still had keys to my house was still really playing on my mind – not because I thought he would break in or anything, but because it was unfinished business. I also knew he would be going away to film *The Jump* and that would make it difficult to get them back. So I sent him a text saying: 'Hi, how are you? If you don't mind just dropping my house keys into Fusey, that would be great. Best of luck on *The Jump*, sure you'll be great.' He sent a really nice one back saying no problem and sending me a picture of his key ring, which was still covered in all the charms we had collected together. It was bittersweet really – when we spoke like that, I missed the old Joey I fell in love with. He was sweet, loving and kind. It was such a shame that he went AWOL.

Our first Christmas with Nelly was amazing – being around a baby brings back all kinds of Christmas memories from when you were small. For me it is doubly exciting as my birthday is New Year's Eve, but Christmas with a new baby is the most magical experience. It was wonderful to see little Nelly and her massive pile of presents, which was twice the size of her! In the evening we had some friends round too and carried on the party. Nelly loved all the attention. She is such a chip off the old block and loves an audience. Poor Greg doesn't stand a chance surrounded by all these Faiers genes!

I was so impressed with all that Billie did. She made it so special and she made sure I woke up there on Christmas morning so I didn't feel lonely. She really looks out for me and since having Nelly, she has become so maternal, which is lovely to see. I think she knows that whilst I am loving being single, it can be a little bit hard during times like Christmas so she made sure I was fully a part of it with Nelly. It was so lovely to wake up there and open our presents all together. I've always been a sucker for the build-up to Christmas and my overriding memory is getting an amazing Barbie house. In the build-up, it had been all I could think about – I saw it on TV in the adverts and in magazines and catalogues all the time – I was obsessed! When I unwrapped it, I went mad and said it would always be the happiest day of my life! This year brought all those good times back and seeing Nelly surrounded by love and gifts made me realize how much I want the same for my children.

Epilogue

So much has happened since I wrote my last book – in true *TOWIE* style it has been full of so much drama, even I couldn't keep up with what was happening next! But, without sounding too deep, I do feel that I have grown to understand myself more and have realized what makes me happy.

I am a great believer in the fact that you can't love anyone until you fully embrace and love yourself, so that's what I am trying to do. I am more focussed on my well-being and my work, although I would be lying if I said I didn't want the 'happy ever after'.

Minnies goes from strength to strength. At the end of 2014 we opened up a new branch in Beverley, Yorkshire, and it is almost a replica of the one in Brentwood – it is down a small pretty cobbled street just off the high street and stocks exactly the same lines as the Essex branch. We thought long and hard about expansion and when the idea was firmly passed by us all, we then thought long and hard about where to open it up and, after lots of market research, Beverley was our place. It is a beautiful market town, full of historic buildings and cobbled streets, and has lots of small-town charm, a wealthy clientele and the main thing is that there aren't that many options for shopping in bespoke boutiques, so Minnies stands a real chance of becoming the 'go-to' shop for both everyday wear and special occasions. It started out smallish – we have two staff in during the week, as opposed to Brentwood where we have one or two staff members in the week, four people at the weekend (six if me and Billie go in) and four people in the head office. For our work Christmas party it was unbelievable to think that we had twenty people round a table – it felt like a real moment for me, Mum, Billie and Libby. We are so proud of what we have done and how we all work to keep it growing.

I feel quite confident that the other things I do only help to promote and enhance Minnies too – all the exposure me and Billie get helps to drive people to the website or encourages them to visit the shop, and the fashion, health and beauty area is where me and Billie feel really comfortable. So, going forward, I am happy to say I have more ranges in the pipeline – swimwear, more clothing and a fake tan range, not to mention being contracted for three more fragrances too. It is the stuff of dreams. Billie and my sister-in-law Hayley having her new shop next door to Minnies is brilliant too as the customers cross between the two stores if they have kids and it is the best of both worlds for us.

After the huge success of the first fragrance La Bella, the owners of Per-Scent were in talks with me about the next products I could look at – we talked about fake tan, make-up and various cosmetics and I loved all those ideas, but I was adamant that it had to be lashes first. It really is no exaggeration that I have wanted to do it for years. The trichotillomania has meant that I've needed smart and affordable solutions to losing my lashes and needed proper bulk where there wasn't any. I have been wearing fake lashes since I was sixteen and have become a total expert in disguising how little hair I have there to cover in mascara. I am thrilled and proud with how they have turned out. Everyone I have given them to has been full of compliments about how light they are and vowed never to go back. I feel this is an area I can really have some authority in. I have tried every single lash that is available on the market and it is no exaggeration to say that I have spent thousands of pounds trying to find the perfect fit, colour and tint, and then this arrives and it is just perfect. The first meeting was in the early autumn of 2014 and we got straight to work on 'Lashes by Samantha', mapping out three styles:

1. Oh! So Natural – is a very chic addition to your daytime make-up.

2. The evening lash that we called If Looks Could Kill – this was designed to create more volume for an 'elegant, seductive look'.

3. Glam It Up! is for the super-glamorous woman who wants to go out there and make a statement. It is what I call the Saturday-night-out lash.

They went on sale at the end of November and sold 900 pairs in just over a week, but the actual official launch didn't happen until the start of 2015 when they went on sale in all leading supermarkets, and then the numbers looked even better. I was amazed that a product could do so well before it officially launched!

I think that one of the reasons why they're so popular is because the base is a gel strip rather than an acrylic one, which means they are so much easier to use. The lashes have a latex-free eyelash adhesive because latex can sometimes irritate the eyes. I also think part of their overwhelming success is down to the fact that I was involved in every detail. I am fully aware we all have different skill sets, but there is nothing I know better than the difference between a good and a bad lash! This is a perfect project for me and it feels good that my condition, as difficult as it can be to live with, has meant that I have this opportunity to put something amazing on the market. I see it as being able to do something really positive, which I would have been incredibly grateful for in my younger years when I felt really alone with it all.

Then there is the other thing that matters most of all to me – my health and fitness. In January this year I launched my new bespoke website: Celebrity Training with Sam, a website about being fit and strong, and having a happy mind. It is a bespoke service that I have helped devise as someone who has struggled in the past with fluctuating weight. It is really weird for me as I have, in effect, grown up in the public eye. If I look back now at photos of me, even from 2012 when

I did my first book, I genuinely don't recognize myself – my face, hair and body are all so different. I know that is growing up and having been ill beyond my wish and my control, but it is also from taking charge of myself.

It is so hard when you are on a show like *TOWIE* to maintain any kind of routine and regular eating patterns – you basically grab what you can, when you can, and most of the time it is crap. Then there are the early starts and late finishes and the late starts and early finishes, which means eating rubbish and drinking loads all day long. No wonder I put on so much weight and felt so sluggish all the time. The truth is that every girl knows their weight goes up and down – for me when I am settled in a relationship I eat far more than usual and put the weight on by eating boy portions of dinner, and in the winter I used to want to get cosy in the onesie rather than go to the gym. Also, without sounding like I am preaching (as I still like a drink), alcohol bloats you full of calories and one of the plus sides of the Crohn's is that I cut wine right out, so felt much better but also lost the white-wine tummy. It was hard to fit in the gym around filming and, without getting all Angelina Jolie on you, it did get harder the more recognizable I got to have a quiet workout with no fuss.

So, with all of that in mind, I have helped to devise a full 360-degree workout website with all different levels of fitness taken care of, as well as being packed with nutritional advice, which you can access from wherever you are. So say, for example, you only like doing cardio exercise and have a sugar allergy, you would create your own profile with that info and the programme would come up with bespoke diet and fitness plans to suit your needs. Your profile is saved and then every time you log into it you recall all your saved info and consult one of the approved experts – Nicole Attrill or Luke Hayter – and keep personalizing to keep pushing yourself. You make your own programme, shopping lists and favourite exercise lists, all for a £12 a month subscription. It is available to have on smartphones or laptops or as an iPad app.

There's been some press saying that I've fallen out with Lucy Mecklenburgh, and it is true that her team unfollowed me on Twitter after I launched my online fitness business. All of us Towie stars have our own business projects and the way I see it, it's all healthy competition. I was the first one to launch my own shop, and then other people from the show, including Lucy, launched their shops, but I just thought the more the merrier. Friendship is really important to me and I've known most of my best girl friends for a long time. Lucy and I have known each other for ages and I wish her all the best.

I just continue to feel blessed really. I have got my contract with Select Models, which has opened so many interesting avenues for me and has helped me have some real clout in the fashion world, and then the Celebrity Training with Sam encapsulates my whole ethos about health and well-being now that my Crohn's is under control. Once I was diagnosed, all I wanted was to feel good and well, and I will do all I can to stay fit and healthy as I never want to go back to feeling as awful as I did. Ever. It was a wake-up call to know that without your health, you are nothing at all, and there isn't a truer statement out there. We are all guilty of taking it for granted and I never will again. It makes me feel more fragile now – the idea that it can all go wrong for you just like that and without warning – but at the same time I am determined to carry on through and not be a slave to it. I will continue to do all the things that I need to and take the medication I need to take, but I won't let it stress me out or become a different person. No way. I have it and I will deal with it.

I feel like I have lived so much already. I think that is the drama of reality TV for you! Everything is so intense all of the time and the months are carved up into filming schedules right at the start of the New Year and that's your year gone in a flash when you see it set out like that. I used to be so depressed and just look at it thinking of all the things I couldn't do.

I do still watch *TOWIE*. I hardly recognize anyone, but I do watch it and I feel so happy to be out of the drama of it all. It is weird living in Essex, where it is filmed and where so many of the cast live – you can walk down the street there and every other person who passes by is easily a friend or a friend of a friend. That said, I have always had a core group of friends and that friendship doesn't change if you are genuine. People forget we all met when we were younger, not on the show. We go way back and it is hard to live in Essex if you have fallen out. Saying that though, there are plenty of people

I don't speak to any more or want in my life. Jealousy is rife in Essex and it can be properly poisonous. Life here can sometimes feel like an endless competition and I am just not interested any more and now I am not with Joey it is easier to step right away from the circuit and live a normal life. Billie is still in the show and has no plans to leave, so I still have that connection, and I have my real friends – they know who they are and, more importantly, so do I.

As for Joey and me – we have definitely both moved on. I've heard and read that he's been with a number of different girls over the months since we split and I wish him well if that's what he wants to do. The last I heard he was trying to hook up with a Pussycat Doll, I think Ashley Roberts is really pretty and I hope things work out.

As for me, after I split with Joey, I knew I needed time and space to get myself back on track. It was only once I finally made the decision we were over, that I could see the relationship for what it had really been – made up of some good bits but, by and large, fairly toxic. I knew it wasn't healthy for either of us, we did something to each other that seemed to bring out all our worst bits, like a negative chemical reaction.

So I threw myself into being single, and I loved it. I think coming out of any relationship that doesn't make you happy is a real moment of liberation, but coming out of one where you've been controlled without realising it, well, it is a real line in the sand. I could drink what I want, see who I wanted, wear what I wanted. But more importantly, I could rediscover the old Sam, the carefree one who loved a laugh and a joke, who was loyal, but was independent and knew what she wanted. I had buried her somewhere in the attempt to be the Sam that Joey wanted me to be. I had changed without noticing and wanted to get me back.

The sole aim after we spilt was to be single and mingle! I didn't want any drama or a boyfriend at all. I was so busy with the clothing, the lashes and setting up the fitness site, I wanted to give it all my full attention. I won't lie, I loved those first few months, I felt strong, healthy and in control of every area of my life for the first time in a long time. I threw myself into my exercise regime, but this time in a good way. I remember my mum saying to me one day: 'I've got my Min back, at last. I knew you were still in there'. Others always notice more than you do when you're in the thick of a hard time, that's why I love my mum, she always lets me find my own way and never nags. We have always been close, but we got even closer once I'd finished with Joey. It really was family time. After work, any spare time I had was spent with Billie and Nelly and seeing the girls again, life felt so good.

They always say that love comes along when you least expect it and I never believed that until I met Paul. In fact, you could say, more than not looking for it, I was actively avoiding it! It was one night at Sheesh and I was out with a big group having a laugh. Actually, it was Billie who had arranged a girls night out to celebrate my newly single status. We decided to get all dressed up and hit the town. I clocked Paul at the bar, he caught my eye immediately and we got chatting and had a bit of a flirt. He was handsome, sophisti-cated and a real gent, refusing to let me buy drinks. I liked the fact he was polite, quiet, almost a bit shy, but still made it obvious he really liked me. We hit it off that night and sort of haven't really left each other's sides since.

I love that he's his own man, he's successful in his own right, really mature, he's not a loud mouth or attention-seeker or a big drinker. Most importantly he loves and respects me for who I am but still wants to look after me. He's so different from Joey in every way and I knew early on it had potential to be serious. It just works, he's normal and has no wish for fame, he's not even on social media! He's a genuine, down to earth guy who works hard for a nice life. We have been dating since last November and I'm so happy. It was no big secret but I just had no wish to flaunt it to the press, I was desperate for something just for us. I've been there and done the 'head-line romance' and I don't recommend it, believe me.

We became pretty serious quite quickly and he met the family early on, there's no getting away with it in my family! I felt really relaxed about it actually, like you do when you know someone is really good for you - I knew they'd agree with me and I was right.

My mum loves him! I think what she loves most is that he is a strong man who supports me but will look out for me too. It is funny really, mum has spent so much of her adult life on her own, with Dad in prison. She's so together and strong but I know she's missed someone to shoulder the bur-den or just take charge. That's what she loves so much about

Greg, she knows whatever happens, his priority will always be to make sure Billie and Nelly are loved and looked after. They are his number ones and mum feels so happy and relieved Billie has that. I know she wants the same for me too and she sees that potential in Paul, of me having a proper partnership where you both look after each other equally. It is weird but Mum is starting to date now that her and dad have split, so it is exciting for both of us to be at a similar stage with things, everything feels fresh.

Anyway, enough gushing! I should know better than anyone that you never know what's round the corner when it comes to love. All I can say is that, at this moment, we are very happy and have just got back from a trip to Dubai and had a wonderful first Valentine's Day together. The future is an unknown thing, who knows what will happen. I am wary of the 'for ever' tag, I thought I had that with Joey. I am determined to take it as it comes. All I can say is that me and Paul will be together for as long as we are both happy, in love and having fun. That's all we can really ask for, isn't it?

On the health front, I have got on top of the Crohn's and phase two of remission came and went without too much drama. I've taken regular medication to keep the inflammation firmly at bay and over the past year I've been researching natural ways of helping with this too. I now include lots of anti-inflammatory foods in my diet, such as oily fish, berries, nuts and brightly-coloured vegetables, and I try to avoid pro-inflammatory foods like refined sugar. For me it is all about health and happiness. It sounds obvious but when either of those is threatened, it makes you all the more determined to hang on to them when you do finally find them. I look back and so much has changed and evolved – I am so different both physically and mentally. I really do realize what matters and I'm happy right now. Fingers crossed I'm lucky enough that it stays that way.

A day in the life of the new me

I've had a lot of stick for my changing shape, which is what happens when you are in the public eye, but I want to be clear – I am not slim simply because I have Crohn's. I was so ill I never thought I'd be well again – and that was my only priority. I would have done anything at all required of me to stop feeling so awful and be myself again.

- Before I started my programme, Celebrity Training, the only important thing was to put on weight in a healthy way. Once I felt stronger, I started to try and build and tone my body. It is unfair of people to say I only have this body through Crohn's – you don't get abs or any kind of definition through being ill, you get it by working hard and taking great care of yourself.

- My diagnosis was a massive wake-up call, when you have been ill, all you want is to feel well again. I wanted to look and feel good and not be a bag of bones, but when I was ill I couldn't train and didn't feel feminine or body confident, so I took things in hand. All those previous obsessive thoughts about being skinny went straight out of the window, health was the priority.

- With my Crohn's I have to be careful with what I am eating and Celebrity Training has a great healthy-eating expert, Sophie Bradshaw, who recommends the best in healthy home cooking – with a little bit of planning you can prepare delicious meals that are packed with goodness.

- A good diet for me would be: an acai berry smoothie for breakfast, a sweet potato and carrot soup for lunch and a superfood kale and mushroom frittata for dinner, as well as loads of water throughout the day. I love porridge, chicken salads, jacket potato with tuna, vegetables and lots of fish. I am lucky that healthy food doesn't depress me or make me feel like I am depriving myself, I actually prefer eating this way which is why it isn't hard to keep it up.

- When I lost a lot of weight from my Crohn's disease, I wanted to make a change and make sure I was healthy, fit and feminine. My motivation is to show that you can keep your body in a healthy and strong place. This is far more important than what size you are, or if you fit into those skinny jeans, it's about how you feel.

- Pick a workout routine that makes sense for your lifestyle and schedule, don't put yourself through spin classes if you hate cycling, or the treadmill if you have bad knees. Find a plan for you and I defy you not to start to love it.

- Understand that a good workout doesn't always mean going to the gym. You can download all sorts of apps to your smartphone, tablet or iPad, where you can store fitness programmes, menus, workout graphs and meal plans. This can help busy people who are on the go and find it hard to commit to regular sessions at the gym.

- I love interval training – squats, lunges, sit-ups with a kettle ball, push-ups, arm exercises, planks – they are all great. Not only do they tone but they burn fat too.

- I have learned the hard way that everything should be in moderation and the only way I will stay in a healthy place is not to let it rule my life in an unhealthy way. So, if I am having a super-healthy dinner, I will have a gin and tonic. If I am eating something with carbs, I will allow myself a drink, but it will be a gin and slimline tonic or a vodka and Diet Coke.

- If you feel confident and healthy then you are on the right track – in my mind beauty is skin deep. I've struggled in the past to feel confident – I've either been bigger than I wanted to be or I've been too thin. Nowadays I don't stress about being skinny, I just want to stay in a healthy and happy place and I finally feel that I'm there.

Acknowledgements

It is hard to know where to start really, but the first thing I want to do is to thank my fans. I am so lucky to have the most loyal and dedicated fan base. Living out your life in the media can be tough, but don't get me wrong, I am not moaning for one minute! But everyone knowing your ups and downs can be difficult, especially when things aren't going so well. I couldn't have done it without you all – you've supported me every step of the way since I left *TOWIE*, since my Crohn's diagnosis and through the split with Joey. But I've also been able to share the good times – the launch of Very.co.uk, the eyelash range, the launch of La Bella and the building of Celebrity Training with Sam Faiers (@CelebTrainSam/www.celebritytraining.co.uk). Whatever I am doing, I know you are behind me and that means more than I can say.

I have a great team around me and they are all family.

My wonderful mum, Sue – you have been the best mum a girl could ask for throughout some of the best and worst times. I couldn't have got through my Crohn's diagnosis without your strength and love. You looked after me so well and were strong when I needed you to be. I love you so much and I am so proud of you for all you have achieved. You are the best mum and nanny and we all love you so much. Dad, thank you for being so supportive and understanding. I love socializing with you and we always have an amazing time. Love you.

Billie – this last year has brought us closer than ever. You were amazing through my illness, strong and loving and I knew you'd make a great mummy, and you are just the best! Nelly is such a lucky girl to have you and Greg as parents – she couldn't be more loved. Thank you for letting me share her life, I can't wait for you to have more!

Greg, thanks so much for making my sister so happy and giving the family our precious Nelly, I can't wait for you to be my brother-in-law.

To the rest of the family, Nanny and Grandad, Nanny Wendy, Grandad Mick, Aunty Libby, Uncle Stuart, Aunty Sam, Uncle Paul, George, Harvey, Teddy, Grace, Eva, Auntie Bongo, I love you all.

To my manager and dear friend Adam Muddle – you are quite simply the best. None of this would have happened without you. We are the best team and great friends and I know you always have my back. Thank you for always having big plans and wanting to 'take it up a gear'!

Thanks to Carly Cook. You have become a great friend and have done a fantastic job with this book. Thank you so much for everything.

A big thank you to Fenella Bates for taking the book on and publishing it so brilliantly. And thanks too to the team at Penguin.

To my girls and gays: Ferne, Sarah, Jerri, Louise, Stacey,

ACKNOWLEDGEMENTS

Steph, Sophie, Gemma Molly, Mark, Benny and Jeff – I love you all and we have so much fun.

My amazing publicist and friend Lauren Lunn Farrow. You are great at what you do and I love working with you. Thank you for all your patience and support.

Thanks to Ian Minton at AM Concepts UK. Thanks also to Julie Minton in Accounts at AM Concepts UK – thank you for all the hard work.

Thank you to Xanthe Taylor Wood (Zante), we have so much fun.

Liv Thomas (Liz) at Lunn Farrow Media, thank you for all the support you give me PR wise you and LLF are the dream team!

Vicky & Saphia from RMI (Sticky & Saucy). Thank you for believing in me so early and for being the best licensing agents in the business. Thanks to Marlisa at RMI HQ as well.

Vipul, Sanjay, Natalie, Tris, Justine, Tom, Daniel & Nisha from Per Scent & The Fragrance Shop. I am so happy to be working with you on such amazing products. Can't wait for the future.

Hannah Witherspoon, Ruth Start, Emma Thorpe, Andrew Roscoe, Louise King & everyone at Shop Direct & Very. Thank you Sandra Foster for making it happen.

Thank you to the team at Lime Pictures.

Ben Taylor and the team at Tour Cloud for always looking after me.

The Minnies Boutique team in the shop and the office – you are all mad but I love you all.

My amazing Glam Squad Lisa Harris, Laurie Hadleigh & Michelle Regazolli.

Karis & Robin Kennedy from Bare Media.

Luke & Nicole at Celebrity Training for keeping me fit.

All the magazines, newspapers and photographers I have worked with over the years.

Picture Credits

Samantha Faiers and family, except:
- Dubai (p. 6): Karis Kennedy
- Sam and Billie (p. 7): Karis Kennedy
- White jumpsuit (p. 9): Ian West/PA Archive/Press

Association Images:
- Big Brother house (pp. 10–11): REX
- Swimwear shoot (p. 15): Matrix Studios
- NTAs (p. 16): David Fisher/REX
- *The Hunger Games* premiere (p. 16): REX